GOOD

BUSINESS

AN ETHICS WORKSHOP
FOR

BUSINESS
LEADERS

JOHN ENDRIS MBA

Printed in the United States of America

ISBN-13: 978-1539989837

Welcome to Your Decision Making Workshop

Why should you learn about ethics theory? Obviously, a business is a complex entity that requires several different factions to function in concert. Basic ethics theory helps to enhance decisions by providing insight into how a variety of people might operate in a complex circumstance. Since ethics theory encompasses philosophy, theology, law, sociology, economics, and psychology, these perspectives can provide an objective framework for analyzing intricate problems.

Business is a network of relationships, so ethical theory is embedded into almost every choice. Studying ethics allows you to examine and articulate your opinions while evaluating other points of view, which is the key to healthy business relationships. Whether you wish to become a leader or just want to follow a good one, understanding group dynamics and a variety of decision-making variables is vital. Plus, how many leaders have you ever willfully followed that could not articulate their justification for a particular decision or strategy? My guess is not many.

Everyone has a unique opinion about what a good decision is, and has their own version of what is right and wrong. However, business choices often have externalities,

3

and businesspeople are often judged on the quality of their decisions, so it is important to be cognizant of how your decisions will affect others. In real time there is rarely ample time to slowly deliberate, so rehearsing decision-making with case studies is good mental practice.

Realistically, approaching the topic of decision making and ethics is theoretical in nature. Since moral issues are dependent on so many variables, any discussion about what ethics is will always be subjective. In fact, there will always be continuous debate about what is considered appropriate behavior. Thus, utilizing basic ethics theories will continue to be a great way to articulate and explain your decisions.

After all of my business training (as an entrepreneur, employee, manager, and student) I have witnessed firsthand how business ethics is often not given its proper place in bottom-line discussions. In fact, I began to notice how having ethical debates in business was comparable to openly discussing religion, sex, or politics in the workplace. It shouldn't be like that. In fact, this was my inspiration for writing this book.

Due to the broadness of this topic, at times the material in this book may seem academic or theoretical, but I purposely made it "high level" to encourage further study. While writing this I tried not to be biased or show my enthusiasm for a particular topic to allow the reader to make their own choices about the content presented. I did my best to be objective and refrain from biased statements or misleading information.

While I developed this book, I struggled with how I

should present other people's ideas and their research. After plenty of deliberation I concluded that it might be overwhelming for the reader and highly annoying if I littered the text with citations. So instead, I have listed the books/academic papers (all of which I got from the public library) throughout and also at the end in case you want to do some auxiliary study and reflection. In fact, some of the concepts are intentionally brief enough to encourage further reading in your areas of interest.

As you will see, I have placed the same interactive case studies in the beginning and at the end, and this was done for a reason. When you read the stories for the first time you should make a gut level decision, write it down, and notate your justification with as much detail as you can. Try not to ponder whether what you wrote is the right or wrong answer. Often in business ethics analysis there are several "right" answers.

At the end I suggest you read through the provided case studies again, and then also jot down your decision and justification. Then compare your cursory analysis and justifications with your post-analysis and justifications. I also recommend assembling a group of three or more people to do the exact same case studies. When doing this, you can share your individual analysis with the group, or try to make a universal group decision with an agreed upon justification. I guarantee that by doing this, you will learn about yourself and also understand how groups actually function when making business decisions.

The first section of the book is entirely dedicated to

individual ethical analysis, and the second half is focused on describing ethics as it pertains to a group. In business, group and individual decision making is sometimes conflated, but in actuality these decisions are quite different. Thus, it is important to take some time to reflect on each separately. The individual section will help you deconstruct how you and those around you make decisions. The group section will help you analyze how groups make decisions.

This book would certainly fit into academic coursework, or function as a supplement, but it is mainly designed with the average businessperson in mind. How a firm or leader responds to crisis and justifies those actions is a major component of every brand and is also critical to success. Thus, this decision-making workshop is designed to enhance operational synergy both on an organizational and a personal level. Ethics and business are often considered separate topics, but often become the exact same thing.

How is ethics and business the same? Since business is a series of relationships that create a functional network, I believe that understanding people is the key to both an effective and profitable existence. So learning ethics theory will inevitably enhance any business relationship. My goal with this book is for the reader to move from reaction to inquiry, to do reflection versus judgment, to strive for imagination rather than imitation, and to look to create dialogue instead of argument.

CASE STUDIES

<u>Initial Analysis</u>:

CASE STUDY 1: "Eminent Domain"

CASE STUDY 2: "Stage Three"

CASE STUDY 3: "Culture Clash"

CASE STUDY 4: "Temporary Fix"

CASE STUDY 5: "Sales Boost"

CASE STUDY 6: "Hot Spot"

CASE STUDY 7: "The Write Off"

CASE STUDY 8: "Free Money"

CASE STUDY 9: "The List"

CASE STUDY 10: "Dumping or Slumping"

CASE STUDY 11: "The Policy"

CASE STUDY 12: "Confidential Information"

CASE STUDY 1:
"Eminent Domain"

Two years ago, Michelle Thompson was elected mayor of Martzville. During this time, Collective Manufacturing Inc. (CMI) left the city, and the surrounding neighborhood called the "Grove" fell into decline. Since the majority of the people who lived in this neighborhood had been employed at CMI the area suffered a high unemployment rate that stagnated after the plant closed.

The housing values in the Grove had dropped and this part of the city became a blighted high-crime area. Due to the frequency of petty crimes, Martzville residents avoided the Grove. For years, citizens who lived in other areas constantly complained to Michelle about the neglected homes and the myriad of societal problems that stemmed from this area.

After another dismal report about this neighborhood and another hopeless community meeting in the Grove, Michelle felt defeated and depressed. Later that week, a developer and a representative from Smart Pharmaceuticals Corporation (SPC) set up a meeting to discuss moving their corporate headquarters to Martzville. During this meeting, several sites were proposed, but the developer and SPC were only interested in the old CMI site in the Grove area.

Michelle left this meeting ecstatic, but still reflected on the disappointing community meeting earlier that day in the Grove. When she got back to her office, she received a call from the developer's attorney. During this call, the attorney reviewed the developer's plans. It was not until this point that Michelle realized the old CMI site was definitely not big enough for the proposed project.

As the attorney spoke about "eminent domain" laws, Michelle knew he was right, and there was no other option. It was true that the US Constitution allowed the government to seize land for "public use" as long as there is "fair compensation." Plus, Michelle was acutely aware of how the property values in the Grove had sharply fallen, and that many of the residents had abandoned their homes and moved to a new city when CMI left.

The SPC headquarters deal would be an opportunity for Martzville to revitalize this dysfunctional area, and bring in new high earning jobs and employees. The new corporate headquarters would add much needed tax revenue and completely change the Grove from a neglected and useless area of the city to a coveted part of Martzville. As the attorney spoke about what was required, Michelle thought over the consequences of such an action.

Deep down she knew the SPC development was exactly what Martzville needed. However, the economically challenged residents in this area would likely receive far less for their property than what they paid for it. Since many of the residents in the Grove would not be able to afford a new house, many of them could be left homeless or even worse.

She took a deep breath and then asked the fast talking attorney to call her back in two days. After she hung up, she stared out of the window and thought over what would happen next. She knew SPC had other cities in mind as well, and the attorney had made it very clear that the eminent domain option was the only way SPC would come to Martzville. Should she move forward with the plan, or deny the project? Why or why not?

CASE STUDY 2:
"Stage Three"

A talented chemical engineer, Puja Wharton left her Fortune 500 job to start her own biotech business. Holding the patent to a new kind of drug, she felt confident her invention would be successful in the market place. After only being in business for six months, her managers were showing her preorders. In fact, the preorders were far more than her small firm could handle at their current capacity.

Even with the patent and a flood of pre-orders, her team still needed to still go through stage three testing. Only after this stage was complete could they get approval from regulators to go to market. This test was by far the most important, and Puja knew that if the drug did not pass, the remaining capital of the firm was not enough to proceed with another round of expensive testing.

A surplus of preorders still continued to flood in as Puja and her team worked day and night to perfect the formula. On the day of the test, the drug failed due to the nasty side effects. Unfortunately, her customer's orders were dependent on approval and the news of the failure would be confidential until the follow-up test.

Puja and her team felt confident that the drug just needed one more small adjustment to pass the follow up. However, it was unlikely that she could afford to pay for another expensive round of testing. If she borrowed the money or got a new investor, there was a chance that the news of the stage three testing failure would go public.

Undoubtedly, her drug would help millions of people if it could go to market. Daily, her managers showed her how eager her customers were about buying the drug, and had even showed her a recent report of a very similar drug coming to market soon. Then they shared the dire financial reports and showed her on the calendar exactly when they would need to file for bankruptcy.

With diminishing capital, her managers presented her with two options. Then they left her alone to decide between the option of selling the company and the patent to a large corporation for two million dollars, or going to Russia to test.

Going to Russia to test would be cheaper and due to corruption her manager assured her the drug would be approved there. After it went to market her firm would make over fifty-million dollars. This money would buy her time to tweak the formula and possibly alleviate some of the unstable side effects. Which option should Puja choose and why?

<u>CASE STUDY 3</u>:
"Culture Clash"

Xavier Rhodes, a poor kid from a working class family worked really hard as an intern and then got his first job on Wall Street. Working as a broker at a major firm was always his dream job, but he still hoped to move up the corporate ladder. Despite his connections from school and the extra hours he put in to get an established pipeline of clients he was continually passed over for promotion.

His expensive Ivy League education had opened some doors for him, but not enough of them to pay off any of his crushing student debt. It was also painful for him to watch the firm that he worked for give out lavish rewards for sales goals, which he rarely ever met. Typically, Xavier skipped lunch to work with clients, but after being prodded by some of his college friends, he finally decided to attend a lunch get-together.

The lunch meeting was cordial, but Xavier grew tired of how most of his friends bragged about their new promotions and higher salaries. He looked around the room and then took a deep breath. Seated next to him was Jack Bilsten. Jack worked at a competing firm across town, but was also an acquaintance of Richard Halstrom, Xavier's boss.

After a few cocktails, Jack pulled Xavier aside and asked Xavier if he would show him the premarket and closing orders of his biggest clients before placing them. If he did so, Jack would route some big orders to him, which would result in a higher commission. Xavier knew that included with the higher commission he would receive high priced season tickets, and two roundtrip plane tickets anywhere in the world. Plus, Jack also promised to help him get promoted.

When the lunch meeting concluded, Xavier and his friends remained, but Jack left and went back to his office. Listening to their boisterous conversation, Xavier discovered how most of them had shared their client's orders with Jack before they placed them. Each of them freely admitted that they now enjoyed a higher salary, and had also gained a higher position in their firms from doing so.

Despite this activity being highly illegal, Xavier was certain no one would ever find out he was sharing the orders with Jack. The majority of his clients were big enough that skimming a few dollars off of the order by letting Jack front-run his own in front of it would not matter. He had never considered this scheme before, but since most of his friends were already doing this, Xavier pondered if this kind of activity was just part of the industry.

On his way to work the next morning, Xavier's phone rang repeatedly, but he did not answer it until the third call. On the other end was Jack. Eager to hear whether Xavier would commit to the plot, Jack sounded impatient. Claiming that he was in transit, Xavier diverted answering the question by saying he would call back in ten minutes. What should Xavier do and why?

CASE STUDY 4:
"Temporary Fix"

Yang Xiong was tired of working as an auditor in a major firm, but he still made an appointment to complete the last test of his CPA certification in three weeks. At his weekly golf outing with his best friend Diego, Yang shared his disgust for the firm he was currently employed at. Diego listened through the long discourse and then mentioned how he was in need of a new CFO.

Yang knew his skills would fit the role of CFO and since he and Diego had known each other since the fifth grade, he immediately offered his services. Without a moment of hesitation, Diego offered him the job. In the span of two breaths, Yang accepted and then called his boss right then and resigned. Yang was as excited as he was intimidated to get to look at the books of Diego's giant firm, and he could not wait to start.

On his first day, Yang met his new staff and got even more excited when he moved into his new top floor office with a picturesque view and posh interior. With a spare moment, he checked his brokerage account. His eyes were instantly drawn to the value of the stock options he had been granted for his new CFO position. When he realized the number was real, his jaw literally dropped. The options granted to him were more than he had gotten in ten years of work as an auditor.

Sitting down at his lavish desk he vigorously pored over the books. Upon his first analysis, some things did not appear right. After further inspection, he noticed several small details did not match, so he ordered more material to be sent to his office, and then he toured the manufacturing facility, the warehouse, and then the document storage room.

After returning to his office and doing more forensic analysis he discovered several entries that were made to mask losses. From there he discovered a trail of entries that indicated Generally Accepted Accounting Principles (GAAP) were being ignored. Digging in further, he realized the manipulation of the books was done primarily as a mechanism to prop up the stock price.

Leaning back in his cozy chair, he stared out at the impressive view and deliberated his options. The entries were layered so cleverly that only one of his former colleagues in all of the auditing firms he had worked at would be able to notice them. When the phone rang he ignored it and went to meet Diego for their usual game of golf.

On the second hole, Yang mentioned some of the accounting irregularities. Diego just dismissed them as only temporary entries kept in place until the firm's sales stabilized. On the third hole, Yang asked a few more questions. When confronted, Diego admitted how these kinds of entries had been ongoing, and had already passed through multiple audits undetected. On the way to the fourth hole, Diego requested that Yang relax and conform until sales got better. What should Yang do and why?

CASE STUDY 5:
"Sales Boost"

Two years ago, Vihan Turner, a tenured manager, was promoted to manage a failing product line, and his company moved him across the country. Despite having to sell his beloved home and relocate, he viewed the promotion as an opportunity, and was eager to make the move. He and his wife both agreed that the salary increase and mild weather would increase their family's quality of life.

Over the last couple of years, his wife and children thrived in the community and were convinced that the new job was an improvement to the quality of their lives. Best of all, Vihan's youngest child was able to finally receive proper medical attention for her disability and see an expensive specialist located in the area.

Everything went well with the new job except each day Vihan was faced with the same lagging sales problem as the previous manager. Throughout his tenure he struggled to fix this pervasive problem, and tried several tactics, but nothing worked. Since Vihan's job depended on the success of the product line, every day he sought out options for a remedy.

After receiving another stern warning from the corporate office, Vihan began to aggressively interview candidates for several recently vacated sales positions. He hoped to find an all-star sales guru who would revive sales and inspire his existing team. Due to his age, he felt that if he were fired, finding a comparable position would be hard. Not only would he need to downsize, his child's medical condition would likely worsen without company subsidized health care.

When the last candidate, Amir Madani opened his briefcase he winked as he put a business card on the table. With a quick glance he noticed a recognizable government official's name on it. Before he could inquire, Sam proposed a scheme that would likely increase sales. Vihan was acutely aware of how certain markets were off limits due to sanctions, yet Amir promised he could get access to them through bribery. Vihan knew the untapped market had enough demand to solve his sales problems and appease the corporate office.

While Amir explained how his bribery scheme would transpire, Vihan listened and pondered. Then Amir proposed that Vihan hire him at an entry level salary, but give him exclusive access to all of the commissions derived from the sales in the untapped market. Everyone believed the ban was unjust and limited the freedom of the individuals in the region. It was only a matter of time before the sanctions were eventually lifted.

Vihan knew how the off-limits region needed his company's product, and how badly Amir needed a job. Vihan also knew that the corporate office would relax and let him keep his job and health benefits if he increased sales. Although he would have to set up a reoccurring bribe to maintain access to the off limit country, he would definitely not get fired. Should Vihan hire Amir and go through with plan? If so why? If not why? What should Vihan do?

CASE STUDY 6:
"Hot Spot"

As a new restaurant owner, Jon struggled. In fact, business was so bad, and his debt was so high that he would have to sell his house to fund the failed enterprise for a few more months, or just consider closing. When Stan, an experienced former restauranteur was hired as head chef, Jon's faith was reinvigorated as he was inspired by Stan.

Over the next few weeks, Stan's impact was obvious. The culture of the restaurant had completely changed, business had picked up and there was clearly a new local buzz about the restaurant. Things were happening fast, and revenue was growing just as quickly. In just a few months, Jon was nearly out of the red, and the restaurant was packed every single week.

While Jon pondered how he might promote Stan, he overheard two customers talking about one of his competitors, the Grotto. Apparently, the chef at the Grotto had hepatitis, and if word got out of this it would negatively affected the business. Then later that day, Stan's ex-wife came in and pulled Jon aside.

In this private meeting she revealed how Stan had

contracted hepatitis, and she explained how his affliction was the catalyst for him closing his own successful restaurant. Whether this was true or false, this was a serious accusation. Before the start of Stan's shift, Jon had originally planned to award him the promotion, but now he was pensive.

Rather than meeting privately with Stan, Jon refrained and instead he went for a walk. Jon was acutely aware of how Stan was the catalyst to his new found success and was the savior of his restaurant. If he were not there, it would definitely be a morale blow to the staff, and since many customers asked for him, it would be difficult to explain why he was not there.

Jon thought about how he would feel if he and Stan were in opposite positions. Jon felt asking Stan the status of his health, and inquiring about his relationship with his ex-wife, would be awkward, and also highly inappropriate. Stan was a great chef, but he was temperamental, and might quit if he was confronted. After a long walk, Jon reflected as he made his way back to the restaurant.

When Jon realized how Stan had recently taken several sick days, this made him even more nervous. Plus, if Stan had hepatitis he was definitely not eligible to work in Jon's restaurant, and may spread it to his staff and patrons. A block away from the restaurant, Jon stopped and stared up at the glowing sign and exhaled deeply. What should Jon do, and why?

CASE STUDY 7:
"Write Off"

At Steelhammer Utilities, Hazel McNelly had worked her way up from the bottom. Now as a vice president she had her own cost center and was finally in a position to award contracts. She was well respected in the industry and had over ten years of experience with various vendors. Hazel was regarded so highly that she was recently awarded a new office twice the size of her old one.

Hazel was about ten years away from retiring and had built up a nice retirement portfolio, but it was still not enough to allow her to support her current lifestyle. On the side, she had invested all of her meager bonuses for the last five years into Bell Weather (BW), a local company with a listed stock on a public exchange. She felt BW was a great company and appeared to be far undervalued.

On Friday, she received a call from BW requesting a meeting. Typically she would not consider small unproven companies like this, but she thought this opportunity might help BW to achieve greatness. When asked to consider rewarding them a major contract, she left the meeting with the financials in hand.

As an investor in BW, she had seen their public

financials before. Even with an initial glance, she knew there was something different about the documents that she'd been given. After a brief examination, she saw no ability for them to honor the agreement and no feasible way for her firm to use the materials in full capacity. In fact, if the financials they had provided were accurate, BW had become insolvent.

Hazel knew there was potential for the news media to perceive this contract as good news, and since she had a big portion of her retirement portfolio invested in BW, she could probably sell her stock at a decent gain to exit the position. She also knew that after the new financials she had just reviewed became public, BW stock would tank. Either way, it was imperative that she immediately unwind her current position in BW before she was wiped out.

Hazel paced around her spacious office, and deliberated. Even if she awarded the contract and BW could not deliver on it, her successful firm could easily write the uncollectible off as a loss, and there were plenty of other vendors she could get for the job. Since she was a trusted expert at her company and also in her industry, she was certain she would not lose her job. While she deliberated, her contact at BW sent her an email including improved financials, which included the revenue from the pending contract. What should Hazel do and why?

CASE STUDY 8:
"Free Money"

After working for Pressfield Inc. for several years, Rick Colland finally got to be the manager of the sales division. His brother Jayden also worked at the company. Both of the men were excited to discuss this wonderful news. After work, they went out and celebrated the promotion. At the first upscale bar, Jayden was overly generous and picked up the expensive tab.

Reflecting now, Rick felt apprehensive about how Jayden had been buying him lavish lunches, but he had never questioned it. They had so much fun that he ignored his suspicion on this occasion as well. After a night out, Rick drove Jayden home and they reminisced about old times. Once they arrived, Jayden reached into his pocket and handed his brother an expensive cell phone as a congratulatory gift for his new promotion.

The next day, Rick began his day by reviewing the budgets with the controller. When questioned about high expenses Rick asked for time to do the proper research and then explain his findings. Looking over the expense accounts and analyzing the data, he noticed his brother Jayden had the most discrepancies.

Upon further research, he discovered Jayden was buying electronics with the company expense account and then likely reselling them at a profit. When searching through the evidence he was careful and unbiased, but everything pointed to this conclusion. The evidence was undeniable.

Later that week, Rick was sent out of town for an important meeting with a vendor, and on the grueling flight home he pondered about what he should do. When he returned, Rick confronted his brother Jayden. When pressed on the matter, Jayden admitted to buying appliances with his expense account to resell them, and justified his actions.

Considering Rick knew how Jayden would eventually get caught, and it would not be long before his scheme was detected, he pleaded for Jayden to confess. Ignoring his plea, and then adding a twist, Jayden mentioned he had used Rick's password to secretly sign off on the purchases. In shock about what he had just heard, Rick froze up. What should Rick do and why?

CASE STUDY 9:
"The List"

Jim and Tiffany worked as account managers at a local insurance company for three years. The fourth year, they began dating and soon after got married. It has now been five years since they started at the company, and they still work together. Over the span of five years, Jim and Tiffany built a profitable client list and had made a wonderful life together. Nearly everything was perfect, except Larry, their tyrannical overbearing manager.

Midweek, Jim had another big argument with Larry, which led to Jim slamming the door of his office in Larry's face. After a quick phone call, Jim was hired on the spot by a rival company into the same position. His new employer was openly interested in Jim bringing all of his clients with him. Despite this request, Jim reflected on the generous offer.

Guaranteed a big promotion if he could convert fifty percent of his old clients to his new firm, Jim analyzed the coveted client list that he had virtually memorized. If he were to pitch these clients he was sure they would convert and bring their business to his new firm. The problem was he and his wife Tiffany built the client list together.

Realizing his dilemma, Jim decided to petition his new boss to hire Tiffany. His new boss agreed, but unfortunately she did not want to change jobs. When Jim told her he had been in secret negotiations with their best clients, and had already convinced some of them to go to the rival firm, she got visibly upset and nearly left the room.

When she paused to mention how this would probably affect her bonus and could cause her to lose her job, she grew even more agitated. By now, she was so upset that she was shaking, which got worse as she shared how she thought Jim had over reacted to Larry's behavior. Jim was silent as Tiffany admitted her disappointment about his new job at the competing firm. After a big argument, she left angry.

Tiffany had not come home for three days, and Jim was beyond worried. Despite this, his new boss gave Jim an ultimatum. He must convert his previous firm's clients to his new firm, or else he could not work there. Barely paying attention, Jim's mind was on Tiffany.

Jim took the long way home and deliberated over his dilemma. When he got home, Tiffany was there. Overcome with emotion, she admitted her recent marital infidelity to him. After squabbling over who was at fault, they decided to resolve their animosity and discuss their mutual problem.

Without a resolution, Jim and Tiffany went to work the next day. Right when Jim arrived, his boss stormed into his office and pressed him to deliver the client list. Right from the beginning, Jim began receiving phone messages and emails from his old clients to inquire about his services, but he was purposely slow to respond.

Jim knew if he did not deliver the client list as expected, he would be demoted or may even lose his job. Considering how tenuous his relationship with his wife was and how Larry would probably not allow him to go back to his old job, he knew he had to make a decision. Jim left the office early and took the longest possible route home. What should Jim do and why?

CASE STUDY 10:
"Dumping or Slumping"

Before he took a sabbatical and invented the wonder drug Fabion, Elias Robowski had worked in many labs over the years. After his big discovery, he created Robco. Over the span of two years, he created other drugs, but his revolutionary drug Fabion was still by far the biggest seller. The success of this product and his company were life changing for both Elias and his family.

With Robco experiencing such high demand for Fabion, Elias planned to expand production. To confirm his strategy, he hired a market research company to provide him with an accurate market forecast. Just like he expected, Elias received a positive outlook, and every source of data confirmed continued demand. With this news, Elias ordered his factory to produce twice the usual amount of the Fabion.

While counting the increased inventory of Fabion, he was pulled aside by his operations manager. In the private meeting, his manager shared the recent notice from the Consumer Product Safety Commission (CPSC). Regretfully, the operations manager informed Elias about how the CPSC had just prohibited the sale of Fabion. After hearing this news, Elias was livid that this message was not shared with him before he ordered the increase in production.

Once Elias calmed down, the operations manager explained a loophole in the CPSC ban. Other countries' medical communities sometimes have different conclusions regarding safety that differed from the conclusions reached by the U.S. medical community and the Food and Drug Administration. Just because a manufacturer can no longer sell the banned product in America, the product could still be sold in other countries that have not prohibited its sale.

He further explained that some foreign researchers had conducted the same studies on Fabion, but they concluded that only stronger warning labels were needed. His manager recommended that Robco "dump" the recalled product and inventory surplus in other countries or they would need to take a write-off that would damage earnings, stock prices, and employment stability. Since the inventory of Fabion was high, Elias knew that chaos would follow a product recall.

Considering how there were now some serious safety concerns about Fabion, and Robco was holding a substantial inventory of a product that has been outlawed in the U.S. what should Elias do? Dump the recalled product and excess inventory in other countries that did not ban its sale? Or should he direct his operations manager to take the write-off, which would hurt the company's earnings for the next two years, and likely result in layoffs?

Typos

CASE STUDY 11:
"The Policy"

A year ago Pam Ingbretson the human resource director for Triton Inc. hired her nephew. Then a year later she hired her daughter Ellen. HR had a policy that an employee cannot take off more than three personal days a month, and cannot be late more than twice. I was an HR policy to give out points for each time an employee was late or tardy. If an employee got too many points they were terminated. However, this policy was not always followed.

Throughout the year, Pam's daughter Ellen was absent and late on several occasions. Despite Ellen's points getting quite high, she continued to be late, as well as take unapproved personal days whenever she wanted to. Her constant absences and blatant disregard for policy were well known amongst her peers and affected both employee morale and production.

When the holiday season finally arrived, Pam was excited to celebrate her favorite time of year. When Pam logged in to her workstation, she got an urgent automated email reminder. Apparently an employee had exceeded their personal points threshold for the third time and severe action needed to be taken. The name at the top of the notification was her daughter Ellen Ingbretson.

When Pam saw the accumulated points at the bottom,

she immediately went into Ellen's personnel file. Then she inspected the attendance sheet for a while before she keyed down to the threshold number at the bottom. She knew she had the authority to make Ellen's threshold higher or just adjust her points to be under the threshold. Her other option was to follow through with the current policy and terminate her daughter.

Pam stared over at the picture on her desk of Ellen's three children. As a single mother herself she knew exactly how challenging it was to get three children off to school and then get to work on time. There were others in the firm who had a similar burden, but her daughter's plight was unique. Not only did she have three kids to tend to, Pam was fully aware of her daughter's pending bankruptcy filing because she had recently borrowed her enough to pay her mortgage.

The cursor on her screen blinked while Pam considered her options again. If she made Ellen's threshold higher, she would have to do the same for everyone and then send out an announcement that the threshold had been universally raised. If she adjusted Ellen's points to be under the threshold, this may get flagged on the next corporate audit, which would affect her job.

She looked away from the screen as she reflected. If she followed through with company policy and terminated her daughter, she knew Ellen would have a difficult time finding new employment and her financial troubles might further compound. This decision would also have an impact on the upcoming holiday season. What should Pam do and why?

- Can adjust ink her working hours to come in late? Day care at work?

CASE STUDY 12:
"Confidential Information"

Candace had been a manager at Safeco for two years. She enjoyed her job and looked forward to going to work each day. She respected all of the employees in her store because all of her direct reports had been her coworkers before her promotion. However, over time they grew apart, and due to her new position she was not able to attend social events like she had before. Despite this fact she still felt a kinship and was grateful for the group solidarity and teamwork that existed in her store.

Recently, her district manager met with her to discuss the inventory problem in her store. Inventory shrinkage is common in retail, but her store had much higher shrinkage than the typical industry standard, or any other store in the corporate footprint. Candace was aware of this problem, but she had not realized her store had the biggest problem in comparison to others. Before she left the meeting she promised to put remediation methods in place.

When she got back to the store, she put out an ad to hire some security guards as well as some secret shoppers.

After three weeks, she did an inventory count and discovered

that nothing had changed. The shrinkage problem still existed, and was now even worse. Her next remedy was to install security cameras. After a few weeks, she eagerly reviewed the surveillance.

After doing so, Candace discovered her employees were not stealing, but instead were doing other things. Two of them were having a very physical love affair while on the clock, another was engaging in a fraudulent food stamps scam, and another was leaving early and having a coworker punch out for them later. She exhaled deeply, and then examined the records in search of the source of the inventory problem.

While Candace was deliberating a new approach to the problem, she inadvertently discovered how the vendors were shorting her on her orders. She never told the employees they were being filmed and recorded. Since the reason for cameras was to decipher the cause of the inventory shrinkage, she knew she could get rid of the cameras, yet her boss was hesitant to do so. She also had to deal with the issues she witnessed on the surveillance footage. How should Candace approach this with her employees and with her district manager? Should she inform the district manager?

CASE STUDY 13:
"Foreign Agent"

As a youth, Abdi moved to America from Kenya. Over the years he worked several menial jobs simultaneously while he attended school. After graduating with honors, he got a job at LeVain Oil Corporation. When he discovered LeVain needed a representative in Kenya, he jumped at the chance to represent the firm in Kenya.

After he'd met most of the top level executives at the firm, each of them raved about how impressed they were with Abdi's intelligent answers and his stunning business acumen. The vice president of the division even sent a personal note to Abdi expressing his confidence in Abdi's ability to expand their business in Kenya. Even though he got a significant pay raise, Abdi was more excited about moving back home than the extra pay.

After a few months, LeVain did their standard expense audit, and quickly discovered how Abdi had rented an apartment in his old neighborhood, a well-known slum in Nairobi. Yet on his subsidized rent form, a different address in a rich neighborhood was listed. It appeared to the audit group that Abdi was expensing $2000 a month for somewhere he did not live. After reviewing the evidence again, the lead auditor brought this discrepancy to management. After learning of this, all of the managers universally agreed to send a representative to find out more about this issue.

When the representative confronted Abdi about this, he did not hide what he did. He claimed that since most of the other executives expensed at least $2000 a month, he thought he should be allowed to do so as well. He also mentioned how he would be considered a target and be vulnerable to thieves if he actually lived in the more expensive place he listed on the form. The LeVain representative's suspicion was noticeable, so Abdi continued.

He further justified this secondary residence by saying how the extra money from the $2000 allotment compared to what he spent for the apartment in his old neighborhood was enough to send his nieces and nephews to school. When pressed further, he said that by being a successful executive, paying for his family's school was expected of him. When the representative returned and shared this information with the managers, a decision needed to be made. What should the LeVain managers do about this, and why?

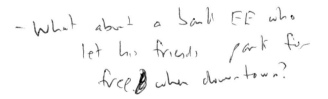

- What about a bad EE who let his friends park for free when downtown?

— I, id easier to make the decisions
when you put yourself in
the shoes of the people or
a more sterile 3rd party
objective position

INDIVIDUAL ETHICS

What are Ethics?

Meta is a modern buzz word derived from the Greek prefix meaning after or beyond. This term is often used to indicate there is another concept added that will complete the previous one. One might use the word meta to describe thinking about what you are thinking, or a self-referential expansion of a concept, or a theory devised to analyze a theory. Why is meta-theory important to you?

In market analysis, examining any preconceived notions is healthy, and just as vital as validity testing. I believe ethics and decision making should be approached in this same objective way. Thus, the individual ethics portion of this book will help you deconstruct your beliefs so you can define your current framework for making ethical choices, yet also understand the components of how other people make their decisions.

Virtually every subject has meta-theory, which is just a theoretical abstract of the topic's properties, foundations, methods, and utility. In any business it is crucial to understand the environment so you can develop a successful strategy, determine the usefulness of an activity/process, or

[handwritten note: This is why reading is so important. Every issue has been written about. Every answer is in a book.]

to verify an assumption. A big part of any business process can be thought of as a series of choices and a network of relationships.

Examining the meta-theory of ethical dilemmas is a great place to start deciphering the complexities of the decision-making process. Being able to examine what went right and what went wrong is crucial, yet this task often happens after the fact. So being able to add some meta-theory before the decision making process is usually quite impactful. Sometimes the easiest way to add some meta can be done by having outside input, or having iterative ideas that evolve.

Despite the advantage of iteration, this valuable process of deconstruction can sometimes be neglected due to time constraints and internal power struggles. Reading case studies in business school and having your analysis picked apart is considered a form of this. This methodology is widely accepted as a way to understand the dynamics of a real business environment. Taking some personal time to reflect, having a mastermind group or even outside council is just another version of this.

Sharing your opinion and justifying it is not always easy. Whether you get feedback internally from self-refection or from an external source, accepting insight of any kind is the cornerstone of a successful endeavor. Before any discussion about ethics can even begin, it is important to start with some critical thinking about the various meanings of the word. Everyone has their own meaning, but what does ethics actually mean?

Is ethics what we feel? Feelings may influence ethical choices, yet simple reactions are not the true arbiter of choice. Feelings are infinite and usually tell us when we did something wrong, but are mostly individual and can be based on formed habits. Is ethics religion? Undoubtedly, people who are not religious can still have ethics, and despite the robust standards set forth in religious texts, not every type of situation is covered.

Is ethics following the law? In some cases it is, but if a totalitarian regime crafted the law, laws may be corrupted. Plus, law is set up to address existing problems and not new ones. Then, is ethics just learning and following culturally accepted norms? Slavery was once a widely accepted norm, but it is always morally wrong. Since culturally acceptable norms change with the times, and may differ from region to region, cultural norms are only relative.

So is ethics science? Technically, the scientific method is a series of repeatable steps that achieve similar results. From the controlled environment's results, assumptions can be made based on the empirical data. Science can explain a situation, but not be useful in telling us what to do. Ethics can be studied in a scientific manner, but cannot be considered a science.

Is ethics your thoughts? Your decision making framework is probably already established. Yet describing the typical framework of an ordinary decision is important. Recognizing an ethical issue is the first step. Getting the facts, and evaluating the choices present usually follows. This basic model is rudimentary and is arguably human nature, but not the only component of ethics.

Some might argue there is a narcissistic quality in self-analysis. There is some truth to this, but self-realization is not at all on the level of a true narcissist who cannot critically analyze their own behavior. Then is ethics actions? When confronted with an ethical choice, biopsychology definitely has a role. Regardless of our thought process, our nervous system is still designed to automatically protect us.

The somatic nervous system is associated with skeletal and muscular voluntary control. The autonomic nervous system controls bodily functions like heartbeat, digestion, and breathing, which are not consciously directed. Unlike our somatic nervous system, our autonomic nervous system is always working. One part of it, the sympathetic nervous system is the trigger for the "fight or flight" mechanism, and the other part, the parasympathetic nervous system stimulates the body to "rest and digest."

Unfortunately, hyperarousal triggered by acute stress throughout most of history has been traditionally handled with either a fight or a flight. I think this feature of humanity also holds true for our modern society as well. In some cases, ethical choices and decision making can be deliberating what you should do and maybe getting hurt, or escaping quickly and safely, justifying what you actually did later.

In his book, The Art of Happiness, the 14th Dalai

Lama said that what completely separates us from animals is the ability to make choices and not exclusively rely upon our instincts alone. As humans, it is a shortcut to blame our instincts for fleeing a stressful situation or making an unethical choice. Actions or inactions are not ethics, and just a part of the bigger equation.

So after all of that discourse, is ethics still undefined? Since ethics theory is constantly evolving, the meta-theory that surrounds it will always be a cause of fascinating debate. Really, all of the variables described influence decisions when combined with a sequence of choices, situational awareness, and societal pressure. Overall, the quality of a decision is what ethics are defined by, and the topic of the next chapter.

REVIEW:

<u>Meta</u>: Another concept added that will complete the previous one.

<u>Meta-theory</u>: A theoretical abstract consideration of any topic's properties, foundations, methods, and utility.

<u>Somatic Nervous System</u>: Skeletal and muscular, voluntary control over your body.

<u>Autonomic Nervous System:</u> Controls bodily functions like heartbeat, digestion, and breathing which are not consciously directed.

Norms:

<u>Injunctive Norms</u>: Behaviors which are perceived as being approved by others (and yourself)

<u>Descriptive Norms</u>: What you actually did and how you behaved in the situation.

Decision Making

Undoubtedly, all decisions are influenced by perception, conditioning, circumstance, and state of mind. Psychologist Leon Festinger uses the term, cognitive dissonance to describe "the mental stress or discomfort experienced by an individual who holds two or more contradictory beliefs, ideas, or values at the same time, or is confronted with new information that conflicts with existing beliefs, ideas, or values." Once you learn how cognitive dissonance can influence decisions, you can use tool to help analyze decisions.

While participating in any kind of critical thinking activity, new ideas may challenge old ideas. In some situations this can be healthy, and in others it may be destructive. Cognitive dissonance theory is founded on the assumption that individuals seek consistency between their expectations and their reality. To do this, people engage in what is called dissonance reduction to bring their cognitions and actions in line with one another.

To temporarily or permanently reduce cognitive dissonance, the options are to change behavior, add a new cognition to it, justify the behavior, or deny the conflict with existing beliefs. Nearly everyone can think of a time where they had to cope with an unpleasant situation by having to do one of those things. Cognitive dissonance is common, but often not recognized.

Fortunately, cognitive dissonance is a topic that has been studied and researched in great detail. Much of the research on cognitive dissonance takes the form of one of four paradigms: the belief disconfirmation paradigm, the induced-compliance paradigm, the free choice paradigm, and the effort justification paradigm. After reading about them here you will certainly know of at least one situation where one of these paradigms occurred.

The belief disconfirmation paradigm occurs when people are confronted by information inconsistent with their existing beliefs. Rather than change their belief and restore consonance, rejection of the new concept occurs by seeking others who support the opposing belief and attempt to persuade others. "Guru-ism" can take several forms and is present in all cultures.

A perfect example is in Leon Festinger's book, "When Prophecy Fails" when he describes how cultists who are programmed to believe in a sequence of events that never transpires, just change their interpretation of the original misperception rather than assimilate the new conflicting idea. Thus, they reinforce the old, unfounded belief instead of confronting the new, fact-based idea. The belief disconfirmation paradigm is widely known, but often hard to

↪This leads to unethical behavior

recognize.

The induced-compliance paradigm occurs when an external force regulates an individual's attitude. A small reward may have some influence on a decision, but a large sum given continuously will breed internal justification for conflicting ideas. Thus, lessening the dissonance and bringing comfort to ideals that the individual may not normally agree with or accept.

Doing work that is unpleasant, but receiving a reward to do so is the cause of this kind of dissonance. Society is filled with induced paradigms, and this kind of dissonance occurs in every aspect of life. Merill Carlsmith, Leon Festinger, and Elliot Aronson, the creators of cognitive dissonance theory have done documented experiments related to this paradigm. Capitalist injustices are often classified as an example of induced compliance.

The free-choice paradigm occurs when an individual is presented with two choices of equal value or appearance. After selecting one, the person will justify and rate the choice they made to offset the feelings and aspects of the rejected choice. Like all choices, this paradigm also can be influenced by groupthink and social pressure.

The idea of justifying a decision is commonplace and alleviates what most people in business call analysis paralysis. Justifying a choice is healthy, but can be taken to extremes for both good and bad decisions. Being forced into a quick choice, may promote this kind of dissonance. Nearly everyone can think of a personal example of the free-choice paradigm.

The effort justification paradigm is dissonance aroused when individuals voluntarily engage in an unpleasant activity to achieve some desired goal. The activity may be something unpleasant, embarrassing, or difficult. Individuals participating in the disagreeable activity often exaggerate the desirability of the goal to alleviate the cognitive dissonance.

Some types of initiation or social-proof activities are usually associated with this type of paradigm. Again, this kind of dissonance is present in many daily activities. The helpful catch phrase "no pain, no gain" sprouted from this kind of self-convincing cognitive dissonance. This type of dissonance is sometimes necessary to undertake difficult tasks.

Regardless of circumstance, enhanced perception and ethical behavior is still an expectation of all leaders. Most would agree that the foundation of ethics is accountability and not excuses. Realistically, in all aspects of life, accepting responsibility under adverse circumstances is a coveted leadership characteristic/quality. So, in theory a circumstance cannot ever be responsible for your outcome unless you avoided making a decision or were not enabled to do so.

When making any decision, if your perception is clouded by dissonance, and you are unable to self-reflect or behave ethically because of it, this is technically an excuse and not a justification. Understanding the elements of cognitive dissonance is important, but mental state cannot wholly be responsible for poor ethical choices. However, being agitated or unbalanced does affect choices and can impact outcomes. So, it is relevant to ask if self-image plays a role in ethics.

Essentially, how you see yourself plays a giant role in cognitive dissonance, but there is much more at work than your self-image. What you wish to be seen as and what you are really seen as is dictated by personal decisions and interactions. Realistically, how you think you are is a past tense version, and how you are perceived by the people you interact with is the present tense version. Every individual is really just in perpetual evolution.

Ethical decision making is sometimes based on normative theory. Normative theory is an ideal, standard, or model, and there are two main ways to describe norms. Injunctive norms are what you should do (approved by society), and descriptive norms are what you actually did. Therefore, understanding the difference is the key to properly defining any situation and objectively analyzing the outcome.

So how do actually you see yourself? In a paper called "Self-Discrepancy: A Theory Relating Self and Affect" Tory Higgins claimed individuals have three selves they compare themselves to. The actual self is made up of the attributes you believe you possess, the ideal self comprises the attributes you would like to possess, and the ought self is the attributes you should possess. When these self-guides are in contradiction, cognitive dissonance can occur.

Self-image can certainly affect decision making, but

excuses and justification are quite different. Understanding your thoughts and previous responses is the thing that ties feeling and action together. Essentially, all of the elements definitions thus far are equivalent to just one thing, self-reflection. Having self-controlled, not situationally controlled behavior typically separates the leader from the group member.

In economics, the term externality is a cost or benefit to a party who did not choose to incur the cost or benefit. Since business is just a series of decisions that lead to an outcome, there are typically externalities involved with most choices. The input of most decision making is a combination of feelings, religion, law, cultural norms, science, actions, perceptions, and thoughts influencing a state of mind or circumstance. The output is usually some kind of externality.

Metaphorically, try to view decisions like an open field that can become anything. Then envision each choice as either a black or a white seed that can be planted. Planting the black seed is the easy choice, which could eventually become a thorn that will need to be justified later. Planting the white seed is the more difficult choice, but it could typically end up as is a beautiful flower or a bountiful food source that will seem like magic later. Being able to realize when there is some form of cognitive dissonance occurring is key to a bountiful field.

REVIEW:

<u>Cognitive Dissonance</u>: Mental stress or discomfort experienced by an individual who holds two or more contradictory beliefs, ideas, or values at the same time, or is confronted with new information that conflicts with existing beliefs, ideas, or values.

<u>Dissonance Reduction</u>: Done to bring cognitions and actions in line with one another.

<u>Externality</u>: A cost or benefit to a party who did not choose to incur the cost or benefit.

Four Paradigms of Cognitive Dissonance:

1. The belief disconfirmation paradigm

2. The induced-compliance paradigm

3. The free choice paradigm

4. The effort justification paradigm

Norms:

Injunctive Norms: Behaviors which are perceived as being approved by others (and yourself)

Descriptive Norms: What you actually did and how you behaved in the situation.

Normative Theory

In ancient Greece, there were two dominant ethical philosophies, Stoicism (300 BC), and Epicureanism (307 BC). Exactly how does ancient philosophy relate to business or help you analyze decisions? These modes of thinking still have an influence today and helped plant the seeds for thinking about externalities, injunctive/descriptive norms, and also normative theory. In fact, these ubiquitous philosophies are the foundation of modern ethics theory and the focus of this chapter.

Do you use your free time to learn new things or to celebrate the luxuries of life, and which do you do more often? Certainly there is plenty of middle ground, but these two philosophies are undoubtedly a major foundation that society is built upon. Do you see yourself as a Stoic who strives for virtue and wisdom to obtain happiness, or as an Epicurean who strives for the highest forms of pleasure obtainable? Obviously, neither philosophy is completely virtuous or useless.

The Stoic was cerebral in nature and attempted to become a clear, unbiased thinker by relying on formal logic and the study of matter in a methodical way. A Stoic was self-contained and created a fortress of inner strength that could not be swayed by the impermanence of troubling events. The Stoic philosophy espoused self-control and mental fortitude as a way to overcome destructive emotions, which were believed to be the root cause for unhappiness. This type of reasoning was disciplined both in action and also in thought.

The Epicurean philosophy was physical in nature and advocated that happiness in its highest form was achieved through the removal of physical pain and mental anxiety through indulging in physical pleasure. Fundamentally, Epicureans believed people need the natural delights derived from sex, companionship, acceptance, and love to overcome destructive emotions. Epicureans were attuned to their awareness of their desires and strived to appreciate all of life's luxuries to the fullest. This type of reasoning was about indulging in each moment as if it were your last one.

Even from this brief overview it is easy to see how these two philosophies have opposing views to life and the myriad of choices available. Critics and scholars both could equally argue that Stoicism was designed for coping with bad times, and Epicureanism was a better fit for prosperous times. These ancient methods of thought helped countless generations of leaders and statesmen explore the definition of truth, and the nature of the soul. If you have not already done so, reading more about these philosophies will undoubtedly expand your worldview.

Even from just this basic description it is obvious these two philosophies still exist today in various forms. However, these philosophies are limited to the happiness of the individual and are far less concerned with what we view as morality. In fact, I think neither philosophy fulfills the main criteria of morality, which are justification and applicability. Plus, neither philosophy actually defines moral responsibility.

The term responsibility is somewhat difficult to truly define. Since it is instinctual to react (descriptive analysis) rather than deliberate (injunctive analysis) the anticipated consequences often affect most decisions. Philosophy is definitely a big part of ethics, but normative theory is based on consequentialist or non-consequentialist thinking. So, ethics can once again be subdivided further into either teleological or deontological choices.

Telos is a Greek word for end or goal. Teleological ethical theories describe our responsibilities and obligations in terms of our attainment of certain goals or ends. Essentially, whatever the ultimate goal is, determines the right course of action. Consequentialist theory is teleological because the moral rightness or wrongness of an act is entirely a function of the consequences. For the consequentialist, what is right and what is wrong is strictly based on the consequences. Consequentialist theory has two main paradigms: Egoism and Utilitarianism.

Egoism has the outlook of "whatever is best for me, and works in my favor is the right choice." Any choice that does not have some personal benefit is therefore wrong. Egoism is popular because it is simple and unconsciously primal. Utilitarianism is doing what creates the greatest good and is in the best interest of the group. Utilitarian rationale definitely seeks to produce happiness, but it is a "majority rules" type of thinking. Results based ethics is quite simple and appeals to common sense, and is based on a hypothetical imperative where the goal is more important than filial duty.

There are three main types of teleological thought, act, rule and negative. Act consequentialism looks at a particular action as morally good only if it produces more overall good than any alternative action. Rule consequentialism looks at an act as right only if it results from the internalization of a set of rules that would maximize good if the overwhelming majority accepts this set of rules, and those rules become acceptable in the community. Negative consequentialism believes a person should choose the act that does the least amount of harm to the greatest number of people.

A big criticism of consequentialist thought is that the person's past actions and character traits are just as irrelevant as the fairness/unfairness of the act. Many critics believe if that everyone adopted consequentialism, there would be adverse impacts on society. Negative effects could include a collapse in mutual trust, unpredictable behavior, a strengthening of bias and prejudice toward the family/social group, and overall a more tumultuous existence for everyone.

Non-consequentialist justification is deontological. The word deontology derives from deon the Greek words for duty, which also means science/study. Non-consequentialist thinking is often considered to be more of a "modern" approach where consequentialist theory has plenty of ancient world history as an empirical basis. For the non-consequentialist, the act in itself is more important than the consequences. Non consequentialist theory is based primarily on what is called the categorical imperative.

The categorical imperative just means that one should always act in a way where the action itself can become a maxim/virtue. The main advocate of this thinking is Immanuel Kant. Kantian ethics outlines a universal notion of rights and equality. Much of this justification comes from a duty based paradigm, with the belief that no matter what, all lives are intertwined and one person's actions affect the group.

Deontology is primarily duty based ethics, which often has very little to do with the circumstances or current situation. Again, non-consequentialist thinking puts more emphasis on the action taken to remedy the situation, and limits focus on the consequences of the remediation. There are several branches of deontological thought, but in general there are three main ones: agent-centered, patient-centered, and contractarian.

According to agent-centered theories, we all have an obligation which gives us reasons for action, and we should focus on keeping one's moral record spotless no matter what the cost. Patient-centered deontology is premised on upholding rights, so any act that violates another person's rights without their consent is morally wrong. Contractarian deontology selects morally wrong acts as those which would be forbidden by principles people in a suitably described social contract would accept or would be forbidden.

Critics believe non-consequentialist thinking often takes a stance of going above and beyond what is standard, which has a narcissistic reflection. Another major criticism is how the idea of humanity supersedes rational elements, and deontology does not account for conflicts of duty. The rigidity of static thresholds of fanatic deontology passively suggests an entire society should perish rather than let an injustice pass. Pure deontological theory can breed uncertainty over which duties qualify as the universal ones to follow.

Essentially, both non-consequentialist and consequentialist thought are theories. Either dimension of ethical reasoning is self-reflective, and may not function the same way when applied to a large diverse group immersed in the constant change and conflict that is business at its core. Just like the ideas in the previous chapter, these concepts are simply ways to dissect established thinking processes and help you learn more about the world and people around you.

Critically thinking about your own moral position is healthy. However, even more beneficial is understanding the ethical standpoint of others, which is an essential component to building functioning teams that make good ethical choices. Whether you identify yourself as a consequentialist or a non-consequentialist, this analysis will help any businessperson steer clear of conflicts and set up functional choices for both their teams and themselves.

Without a doubt, the choices we can make have a greater impact on those around us than ourselves. Yet as humans with free choice, we will always be unpredictable. We all have injunctive norms of what we think we should do/what we believe we are capable of and also averse to. We also all have descriptive norms to describe what we actually did, which defines our real patterns of how we actually behave. These useful models are the focus for the next chapter.

REVIEW:

<u>Stoicism</u>: Cerebral in nature, and believed that self-control and mental fortitude could overcome destructive emotions, which was considered to be the root cause for unhappiness. This type of reasoning was disciplined both in action and also in thought.

<u>Epicureanism</u>: Physical in nature, and believed that happiness in its highest form was achieved through the removal of physical pain and mental anxiety through indulging in physical pleasure. Epicureans were spontaneous and attuned to their awareness of their desires.

<u>Teleological Theories:</u> Goals, or ends based ethics, consequentialist motivations.

<u>Deontological Theories</u>: Duty based ethics, non-consequentialist motivations.

Models for Decision Making

How is a decision actually made? Often this kind of analysis is often overlooked. Can you look back and explain exactly why a particular choice was made? Likely it was based on a mix of three things: obligation, personal ideals, and consequences. In other words, what do you owe, what do you believe, and what will be the impact of your choices.

Notice how all of these components revolve around the interpreter? Some decisions involve all three components, while others may just be based on one component. Essentially, these elements make up your ethical choices and define your unconscious decision-making models. These components also form the basis of your intuitive opinion about ethical leadership and character.

How is ethical leadership and character even defined? In the previous chapter, teleology (consequentialist) and deontology (non-consequentialist) were examined as elements in ethical choice. Even though most ethical theories are based on injunctive norms, most case studies are built on the descriptive norms. Once you recognize these models in the people around you, it will help you build much more efficient teams.

Theoretically, there are five established social justice/decision models that most people unconsciously rely on: Mill and Bentham's utilitarian model, Kantian ethics, Ross' non consequentialist model, Nozick's libertarian philosophy, and Rawls' social contract model. You will certainly recognize these decisions models, and will discover that these models will broaden your analysis when analyzing the case studies (and also other people). To refrain from showing any favoritism, none of them are in ranked any order.

John Stuart Mill and Jeremy Bentham developed utilitarianism to address social problems. Utilitarianism is consequentialist theory and the main objective is to always act in the best interest to provide the most good for the most number of people. The utilitarian's model of justice is to select the act which produces the greatest possible balance of good over bad for a selected action. This approach is flexible, has immediate results, and emotion is rarely considered. The strength of this approach is that it provides a clear, straightforward basis for formulating and testing ideas.

A weakness of utilitarian thinking is it assumes the ability to quantify issues objectively, and often entails individual sacrifices to favor the majority. The biggest weakness of this model is that even if an action is morally wrong, if it produces the most happiness then it is the right choice. Some actions are wrong even though they produce wellbeing.

Since each group or individual's personal definition of happiness is what ultimately determines a just or unjust action, the utilitarian choice may not be aligned with accepted cultural/societal norms. If the rightness/wrongness of an action is solely based on its consequences, and the consequences are transferred away, then undoubtedly justification is skewed.

Immanuel Kant is the founding father of Kantian ethics. The non-consequentialist Kantian approach judges that any act is only right if we can will it to become a universal law/maxim of conduct. This model relies on firm rules that do not depend on circumstance, and views everyone as an equal. The strength of this thinking is it depends on acting on principle and not circumstances. Thus, it attempts to put a societal governor on the individual's less than righteous primitive desires and self-centered ambitions. A much higher value is put on duty than on the incident.

The weakness of this model is it is not flexible because and has no comparison for values. Kantian ethics somewhat relies upon the grand vision of equality, which is often considered idealistic. The Kantian ideal of universal rights has now become a feature of a modern international society. Yet the grand dream of creating goodwill as a universal law for everyone is sometimes smothered by logistics.

Although Kantian thought is based partially on both deontological and teleological ethical models, the Kantian ideal has yet to be realized, and is thought of as newer concept in global society. A major weakness/limitations of Kantian thought is how it is defined by terms of duty, it allows no exceptions, and has no way of deciding between competing values.

Briefly mentioned in the previous chapter, hypothetical imperatives tell us which means best achieve our ends, but they do not tell us which ends we should choose. The justice model for Kantian thought is called the categorical imperative. A categorical imperative is an absolute unconditional requirement that must be obeyed in all circumstances and is justified as an end in itself. A moral proposition can be interpreted in several ways, but Kantian thought can have limits on analysis.

Is it okay to steal? If the notion of personal property does not exist, the proposition has negated itself. Perfect and imperfect duties exist, but until they are declared, they are not defined. If one society deems personal property illegal and another defines it, then is stealing okay in one culture and not another? Overall, the Kantian thinker's model of justice relies upon the grand vision of equality and a universal law for everyone may not fit everyone the same.

The libertarian model of justice revolves around the concept that anything which disrupts an individual's freedom, or interferes with personal property or the right to choose is considered wrong. This model was developed by Robert Nozick in 1974 and has a major focus on entitlement. Libertarian thought is based almost entirely on ethical relativism (right or wrong depends on the moral norms of the society in which it is practiced).

A major strength of libertarianism is that it recognizes a variety of moral concerns. Libertarianism acknowledges the legitimacy of organizations, but stresses the rights of the individual over the group. It maintains that people and organizations are entitled to their holdings, and reveres the power of property and personal sovereignty. This theory is grounded on negative natural rights, and since America was founded on negative natural rights issues, this type of thought is sometimes conflated with the "American way."

The biggest problem with this ideal is that people who were endowed with the favorable accident of arbitrarily being born to the right parents or situation can excuse their bad behavior or failure to give relief for a person less fortunate. The libertarian concept is inflexible and egoism fits perfectly into this model. Moral rights are often unique to each person, and some might even be controversial. Often laissez-faire (letting things take their own course, without interfering) can have disastrous consequences. It is often argued that libertarian ideals rarely promote sustainable cooperation among symbiotic citizens.

W.D. Ross developed non-consequentialist moral theory, which is a deontological form of ethics. His philosophy is centered on prima facie a Latin term meaning "at first appearance" or "immediately clear." Ross' list of prima facie duties is, fidelity to your agreements, reparation to make up for any wrongful acts, and gratitude and repayment for past favors. Justice and improving the conditions of others, as well as a duty to not harm them are also included in "prima facie" duties.

Prima facie duties are simple. In cases where only one principle applies, or when more than one principle relates but the principles do not conflict, then determining one's actual duty will be straightforward. The biggest strength of Ross' concept is that an individual is empowered to make rational choices and act upon them. Also, the decisions are based on something other than the consequences. This theory implies that all humans are logical.

The weakness of non-consequentialism is that duties are unsystematic and follow no logical pattern. Some have criticized Ross' prima facie duties list because the duties are done on a whim. Essentially, there is no principle for determining what the actual moral obligations are. Non-consequentialist theory has no tether to universal tenets because whether an act is right or wrong depends on factors other than a strict set of guidelines or relevant consequences. This kind of moral theory relies more on serious thought and reflection than strict adherence to format.

John Rawls is the creator of the social contract thinking. This is non-utilitarian thinking and is morally defined as equality created from a point of empathy. The ideal is based on the concept that not everyone deserves a fair share but they do deserve a fair opportunity. The main tenet is the veil of ignorance as a justice model for decision making.

Behind a veil, everyone is in the same situation and

everyone is presumed to be equally rational. Since everyone adopts the same method for choosing the basic principles for society, everyone will occupy the same standpoint: that of the disembodied, rational, universal human. Therefore all who consider justice from the point of view of the original position would agree upon the same principles of justice generated out of such a thought experiment. Any one person would reach the same conclusion as any other person concerning the most basic principles that regulate a just society.

Social contract thinking is about the equal distribution of civil liberties and social/economic goods as widely as possible. In other words, social contract philosophy thinks it is wrong to not forgo some of our civil liberties in favor of greater economic advantage. Critics describe this ideal as ignorant of the different abilities, tastes, and conceptions of good and bad. Assuming that everyone behind the veil is the same or has an identical view of fairness can be construed as non-pragmatic.

Obviously, when examining any situation the "right" outcome can easily change if you filter it through ethical relativism, teleological, or deontological thinking. Whether the decision is based on a utilitarian model, a Kantian model, a non-consequentialist model, a libertarian model, or the social contract model, the "right" choice/filter can still be equally debatable. Thus, when examining any ethical decision from the group perspective, eliminating any "zero sum game" principles is definitely an excellent practice.

REVIEW:

Ethical Relativism: The idea that ethics are a matter of perspective, where a group, culture, tradition, and background will influence and be the exclusive moral compass one operates with.

Utilitarianism: Greatest possible balance of good over bad for a selected action (John Stuart Mill and Jeremy Bentham)

Kantian: Goodwill as a universal law for everyone (Immanuel Kant)

Libertarianism: Personal liberty, and property rights (Robert Nozick)

Non Consequentialist: Prima facie duties based on rational thought (WD Ross)

Social Contract: Universal equality (John Rawls)

Imperatives:

Hypothetical Imperatives: Tell us which means best achieve our ends, but they do not tell us which ends we should choose.

Categorical Imperative: An absolute unconditional requirement that must be obeyed in all circumstances and is justified as an end in itself.

Decision Making Analysis: Behaviorist Versus Cognitive

Why is deconstructing ethics important to creating a profitable business and functional teams? All philosophy and normative theory just strives to ask questions. Engaging in this kind of critical thinking removes an individual from their comfort zone by making them analyze their own thoughts and perceptions. By defining a problem or issue, it forces the thinker into a reaction or a response. This is where philosophy, psychology and ethics all cross paths. I think analyzing decisions is helpful for everyone, but even more so for business people.

The most widely accepted approaches for analyzing decisions are behaviorist, cognitive, developmental, humanist, personality, social, and learning theory. Yet behaviorist and cognitive theory are the most well-known. Behaviorism is the study of behavior for the purpose of identifying its determinants. Behaviorist theory believes that conduct is governed by a finite set of conditioned responses, and we all are so alike that when presented with certain consequences and stimuli we will react in similar ways.

Cognitive theory attempts to analyze and deconstruct the mental process behind the behavior, which is truly different to each person. Of course, each theoretical outlook has its flaws, and cannot summarize all human behaviors. Some people strongly believe that behaviorism drives our behavior, while others advocate for cognitive theory. This is why I separated the two concepts into different chapters to give the reader a broader viewpoint to use for their own analysis.

Behaviorists believe that our perception can be created or changed through conditioning and social programming and that behavior is simply a product of conditioning with rewards and punishments. In his paper "Psychology as the Behaviorist Views It" John B. Watson based his theories on the idea that belief and behaviors can be measured, and changed through training. This concept is also fundamental to business systems, and ubiquitous in corporate culture.

In many institutions, both business and otherwise (especially the military) there is extensive training and expected social protocol. If you observe any organization you will find conditioned responses, which are intentionally created through a series of negative and positive reinforcements. Some might say the rules and structure that defines an institution help to create and also enforce social programming.

Realistically, neither social conditioning nor environmental factors are solely responsible for ethics, but obviously have an influence on an individual's perception. Perception is continuous, so it is difficult to spend time thinking about the process as we are constantly consumed by the stimuli around us. Despite being constantly immersed in reality, scientists have discovered there are five universal brain frequencies that we all use for mental functioning.

Despite our different personalities and cognitive outlay, gamma, theta, delta, alpha, and beta frequencies are used to define and categorize common brain functions that are present in everyone. Gamma frequencies are used for higher processing. Theta frequencies are used for daydreaming and sleep. Delta frequencies are used for relaxation and rejuvenation. Alpha and beta are the most important modes of daily consciousness, which several marketing studies have utilized to drive daily decisions and analyze predictable behavior.

Beta frequencies are our alert consciousness, where we are perceptive and on edge. Physically, this is identified by rapid eye movements, pupil dilatation, and sometimes perspiration. Mentally, it is identified by a heightened awareness of your surroundings and stimuli. Soldiers are often traumatized from constantly being in this mode. Alpha frequencies are the day to day, muscle memory tasks and could be best described as our "comfort zone."

Remember the autonomic nervous system from the previous chapter? The sympathetic nervous system is the trigger for the fight or flight mechanism, and the parasympathetic nervous system stimulates the body to rest and digest. Many of these common frequencies have triggers that we are mostly unconscious of, but impact our behavior. Most people would not spend even a moment classifying what frequency they are using. Many modes are automatic and unconscious, which is what behaviorism and social programming rely upon.

To prove their theories, several behavioral scientists use longitudinal studies, which involve repeated observations of the same circumstances over time. In some ways, a longitudinal study is not much different from witnessing the developed culture function in any work environment. In any organization, encouraging wanted behaviors and discouraging unwanted ones is where most organizations get their culture from. A big part of business ethics and responsible leadership is to analyze the actions that are being incentivized and encouraged.

Psychologist Henry Murray built his psychogenic needs theory on Abraham Maslow's, famous hierarchy of needs and humanist theory concept of primary and secondary needs. Like Maslow, Murray claimed that people's behavior is motivated by needs, which essentially influences their decisions. Murray's needs categories are ambition, materialism, power, affection, and information. In her book "Self-Analysis" Karen Horney proposed that some behavior is due to a neurotic need for affection and approval.

Most business professionals are acutely aware of how psychogenic needs and neurotic needs motivate decision making. It is quite easy to simplify all decisions and categorize them in this way. However, most complex ethical decisions involve multiple layers of analysis and self-awareness. There are also several situations in business where the luxury of deliberation is not available. In theory, conditioning arguably plays a part in forced decisions, and certain decisions may be expected by the culture of the institution.

Social scientist Albert Bandura is known for his observational and social learning experiments. His theories involve shaping, modeling, and vicarious reinforcement with the belief people can learn new information and behaviors by watching other people. His theories expand behavioral theory by recognizing how the mental state is important to both learning and decision making.

Social learning is not a new concept, anyone who has done an apprenticeship or had a positive role model understands his concepts. Bandura once did an experiment that showed how children's phobias went away when they were around kids without phobias. However, he is far more renowned for introducing the self-efficacy concept, which just states that all people can identify the things they would like to change.

Going back and changing personal ethical choices is impossible, but changing future responses to the same stimulus is not. People with strong self-efficacy view challenges as interesting tasks, form stronger commitments, and recover quickly from setbacks. People with weak self-efficacy will avoid challenging tasks, focus on negative outcomes, and often lose confidence in personal abilities to confront dilemmas. Developing self-efficacy through conditioning is entirely possible.

Social scientists have also done a lot of work on the importance of priming which just means triggering some thought or association in such a way as to affect people's choices and behavior. In longitudinal experiments done on group decision making, engaging participants in a prior task that involves either "getting along" or "critical thinking" has been shown to have a big impact.

When people were given a getting along task, they were silent. When given a critical thinking task, they were far more likely to disclose what they knew. So if the leader of a group encourages information disclosure from the beginning, even if it goes against the grain, members will probably do less self-silencing. This concept is readily apparent in nearly all organizations and has been proven throughout history.

Being overwhelmed by the busy daily regimens of the business world, programmed social conditioning is often overlooked. Scripted responses by the legal and human resources department rarely apply to all situations, yet often become the mainstay reaction. Arguably, behaviorism is not entirely about programming individuals to act in a certain way. It is more about examining programmed behavior to find insights into relationships and norms of an organization or specific culture.

How is behaviorism theory important to business? The environment and culture of a firm, including those involved with it, are a stimulus that affects an individual or a group's collective perception. The environmental stimulus is far too complex to consume all at once, but on the most basic level this aspect is a starting point for cultural awareness. The attended stimulus is what researcher's call the specific objects in the environment that attention gets focused on.

Attended stimulus can be based on familiarity, or novelty. In business, these elements are often unnoticed, but are quite important to the culture and ethics of every firm. Transduction allows visual messages to be transmitted to the brain to be interpreted, and then the signals are sorted into meaningful categories. Then repeated recognition creates action to complete the cycle. Deconstructing a business environment from a behaviorism perspective, will give an astute businessperson a unique insight into how the people in an organization may respond to change.

Behaviorism is not the only component of decision making, nor can it be entirely blamed for judgment errors. Yet it is undeniably a factor. Any great leader will assess the environment they are creating, and observe how the stimulus within it affects productivity and decision making. Behaviorism is interesting because it does prove how similar we all are. Understanding behaviorist theory as a business person will definitely add a new dimension to business strategy, and self-reflection. Plus, being able to deconstruct a specific culture or environmental patterns might make adapting easier.

REVIEW:

<u>Behaviorist Theory</u>: Psychology should have only concerned itself with observable events and theories are supported by empirical data. Belief and behaviors can be measured, trained and changed

<u>Developmental Theory</u>: Psychological approach that aims to explain how children and adults change over time.

<u>Social Theory</u>: Behavior is based on the interactions with others. Social Theory is a combination of Behaviorist and Cognitive theory.

<u>Psychogenic Needs</u>: A theory based on Maslow's concept of primary and secondary needs, which claims that people are motivated by needs, which will often influence their decisions.

<u>Longitudinal Survey:</u> A study that involves repeated observations of the same observations over time.

Decision Making Analysis:
Cognitive Versus Behaviorist

Undoubtedly, social programming exists in everything. However, behaviorism is often criticized as a one-dimensional approach because it does not account for types of learning, personality, perception, social caste, and intelligence, which are present in all situations. Since behavior is observable it is easy to collect data and quantify data, so behaviorist data often becomes common knowledge to create stereotypes upon. Unlike behaviorist theory, cognitive theory is not based purely on responses to external stimulus.

Cognitive theory explores intelligence, personality, state of mind and perception with a focus on individual reasoning. Realistically, people are a collection of multiple identities, and history has shown humans are far too complex to predict. The unconscious mind and other cognitive elements are not as easily quantifiable as behaviorist reactions. Cognitive analysis believes that how an individual filters and develops meaning is a unique mental process that can affect their conditioned response.

Making rational decisions and good choices is a crucial

element in business, and frequently more important than any other factor. Of course, learning cognitive and behavioral theory is not an essential part of doing business, but these theories may help you develop team building skills, and cultivating cohesive ethical choices as a leader. Regardless of any kind of organizational conditioning, or repeatable business model, perception, personality, intelligence, and state of mind are all variables that undoubtedly impact the predictability of social programming.

Jacques Lacan, a controversial, but prominent psychoanalyst and social theorist, was an advocate of the idea that there are two selves/perceptions that are in constant struggle. Lacan's work is not well known in business, but his concepts are probably quite familiar. He claimed that the same person has two identities. Everyone has a perceived by society identity, and an internal self-identity, which must mutually coexist. In the business world, "not bringing your problems to work" is considered professionalism. This ideal is praised, but only strengthens the divide.

In Lacan's reality there are three phases of the psyche the imaginary, the symbolic, and the real. These three dimensions control our desires and determine how we define ourselves. It is easy to speculate how these separate selves could each make different decisions based on the same facts. It is also equally easy to imagine how a business could also have this same identity complex.

According to Lacan, the I is a self-created fictional

creation and is a delusional image that one can almost never obtain. The imaginary domain is how someone perceives their external image, which is often how they ideally want to be and not how they actually are. An idealistic corporate mission statement could be compared to this injunctive state.

The symbolic is the realistic realm of culture, which can be succinctly categorized as the anthropological dimension of life. The real is an argument about the descriptive state of being, and the threatening of injunctive reality. Obviously, not every decision a firm makes is based on their idealistic mission statement, and some might even conflict with it. With businesses or individuals, this same paradox exists. Who makes the decisions? The external or internal image or a combination of both?

When incorporating cognitive theory into decision making, personality certainly influences a decision making process just as much as conditioning does. Defensive mechanisms like neurotic anxiety, a fear of real world events, and moral principle can sometimes be unbeknownst to an individual, but obvious to a group. How an individual might be impacted by externalities or daily events they are sensitive to can also influence their "normal" everyday behavior, which may even result in them making an adverse ethical choice.

Any perceptive business leader knows that regardless of predictable business models, programmed behavior, and quantifiable systems, mood and personality sometimes dictates how operations function. Undoubtedly, intelligence is also a factor in the decision-making process. However, how intelligent someone is can be quite difficult to measure. Since intelligence can take many forms, there is no one way to measure each type all equally or rank the array in any order of importance.

Malcolm Gladwell, in his book "Outliers" claims intelligence has little to do with ability/talent, and that true skill comes from repetition of a specific task. Gladwell believes that if anything is repeated for 10,000 hours, mastery will be achieved regardless of intellect or talent. However, depending on the task selected, intelligence is still a factor. Louis L. Thurstone, Howard Gardner, and Robert Sternberg have all been pioneers in the field of intelligence research. Each of them has a differing viewpoint on what intelligence is and how it can actually be measured.

Thurstone's theory of intelligence focused on defining seven different primary mental aptitudes: verbal, reasoning, perceptual speed, numerical ability, word fluency, associative memory, and special visualization. Similar to Thurstone, Howard Gardner's multiple intelligences theory has eight distinct intelligences: visual/spatial, verbal/linguistic, body/kinesthetic, logical/mathematical, interpersonal, musical, and naturalistic intelligence, all of which are based on skills and abilities universally valued within several different cultures.

Robert Sternberg's triarchic theory of intelligence proposed that successful intelligence is a mix of three factors: analytical problem solving abilities, creativity of using past experiences and current skills, and the practical adaptability to deal with new situations/environments. Undoubtedly, intelligence is relevant to decision making. However, determining an individual's ability to use their intelligence is quite different from determining their ability to make rational decisions.

The variables of personality, intelligence, and perception certainly complicate the simplicity of the programmed reactions of behaviorism. While being immersed in reality, it is quite difficult to dissect and deconstruct all of these variables as they are occurring simultaneously. If any of the five universal brain frequencies we all use for mental functioning is overproduced and/or under produced, it can cause faulty perception. To review, the five frequencies we all rely on are, gamma, theta, delta, alpha, and beta.

Gamma frequencies are used for higher processing and cognitive functioning. If too much is present, this causes anxiety, high arousal and stress. If too little is present, ADHD, depression, and learning disabilities may occur. When the optimal amount is present, information processing, learning, perception, and REM sleep are increased. Meditation is said to increase gamma waves.

Theta frequencies are used for daydreaming and sleep. If too much is present, inattentiveness and depression can occur. If too little is present, poor emotional awareness, stress, and anxiety can increase. With the optimal amount, this frequency is responsible for enhanced creativity, emotional connection, and intuition. Some claim that depressants help to increase theta waves.

Delta frequencies are used for relaxation, rejuvenation, and restorative healing sleep. Unfortunately, these waves are found most often in infants and young children. As we age, we produce less delta waves. If too much is present, severe ADHD and the inability to deliberate is a result. Poor sleep and the inability to rejuvenate the body and mind occur if too little is present. With the optimal amount, the immune system and natural healing are boosted. Most researchers believe that sleep will increase delta waves.

Beta is our conscious thought and logical thinking. If too much of this frequency is present, high arousal, high adrenaline, and the inability to relax will occur. If not enough is present, poor cognition and depression are a result. With the optimal amount, conscious focus, and problem solving are increased. Coffee, energy drinks, and various stimulants are believed to increase beta waves.

Alpha waves are believed to be the gateway to our subconscious mind. Sometimes when we become stressed, a phenomenon called alpha blocking can occur, and there are even prescription pills available for this task. If too much alpha is present, daydreaming and the inability to focus can result. If too little is present, anxiety, OCD, and insomnia can occur. The optimal amount will bring relaxation. Antidepressants like alcohol and marijuana are believed to increase alpha.

Regardless of any programmed actions being a part of

a specific culture, important decisions can deviate from the norm if any combination of natural brain waves is out of balance. Certainly, brain waves are not a viable excuse for a poor decision. However, an imbalanced proportion may influence how much or little consideration was involved in the decision making process. Yet realistically, equally bad choices can be made by deliberating at great length or by making a spontaneous gut decision.

Even if a specific cognitive state is "best" suited for decisions, the individual's perception is sometimes clouded by unconscious perceptual heuristics which may influence their choices. Perceptual organization is how different objects are sometimes erroneously grouped to form larger ones. Mental shortcuts like this are often referred to as mental heuristics.

Everyone can think of at least one time they perceived something as related, and later found out it was not. The (Gestalt) laws of perceptual organization are similarity (similar things grouped together), pragnanz (everything is as simple as possible), proximity (spacial grouping), continuity (creating linear connections), and closure (grouping for convenience). In the overly complex and busy world of business, these heuristics are often responsible for spotting perceived trends that may not actually exist.

Unquestionably, one of the most interesting components of ethics is how there is nearly always competing rights where two ideas are both sound, but different. Having the ability to objectively view competing

84

rights has been proven to be a trait that will inspire those around you. That is why behaviorism conditioning is often criticized for removing, logic, facts, principles, and many other individual variables that influence decision making and moral judgment.

Of course, anyone interested in learning about business ethics seeks to develop a framework for analyzing their own or others' decisions. Undeniably, depending on the amount of prior conditioning, behaviorist triggers have different effects on individuals. However, it is undeniable that cognitive theory has a role in most decision making. Undoubtedly, combining both of these perspectives when analyzing both your choices and others around you will allow you to have a more objective view.

REVIEW:

<u>Cognitive Theory</u> : Concerned with processes which occur inside the brain and nervous system as a person learns. Psychology deals with perceptual organisms, who organize, interpret, and give individual meaning to the events impinged upon their consciousness (Gestalt Theory)

<u>Humanist Theory</u>: Rejects the notions of behaviorism that the environment determines the outcome. Favors the notion that human beings can control their own destiny, are inherently good, and desires a better world for themselves and others.

<u>Personality Theory</u>: The major theories include dispositional (**trait**) perspective, psychodynamic, humanistic, biological, behaviorist, evolutionary and social learning perspective.

<u>Learning Theory</u>: Cognitive, emotional, and environmental influences, as well as prior experience, all play a part in how understanding, or a world view, is acquired or changed and knowledge and skills retained.

<u>Gestalt Laws of Perceptual Organization</u> (Cognitive Theory)

The Law of Similarity
The Law of Pragnanz
The Law of Proximity
The Law of Continuity
The Law of Closure

<u>Competing Rights</u>: Two ideas are both sound, but different.

Working Paradigms

How do you think you are perceived at work? Do you think this image matches how people actually perceive you? At work you do whatever you can to project the image that you think will get you a raise, earn respect from your colleagues, and build strong partnerships. How do you know if it is working? How do you know if what you are portraying is being decoded the way you expect? What if those things are not even what is expected?

Realistically, who you think you are is based on your past history and decisions. How you really are is based on your present decisions. In business, benchmarking performance and preconceived measurable standards is the norm. Arguably, without this, a firm will never know how well it is doing. Is there a benchmark like this for your own viewpoint? How will you know if it is clouded by misperception or if it is aligned with reality?

In the same regard, take a moment and imagine what your firm's culture and familiar working environment is like to an outsider? How would they describe how you interact with your environment? Do you work in an environment where you get this kind of critical feedback? Are there benchmarks in your past that you are compared to? Are there even standards that you can measure your effectiveness against? Or are you only evaluated by your competition?

Formal employee evaluations are often considered negative experiences, and sometimes perceived as an ambush. Depending on the firm's culture yearly review sessions can often be about forcing everyone into the same template rather than harnessing an individual's unique strengths. So the material in this chapter is designed to show you a way to develop your own personal strengths and weaknesses.

In 2005, an academic paper from the University of Michigan called, "Composing the Best-Self-Portrait: Building Pathways for Becoming Extraordinary in Work Organizations" was published. This paper introduced Reflected Best Self (RBS) theory. This paper is expansive and gives the reader many things to deliberate. However, the main topic is about how employees understand themselves to be and what they really are.

Through experiences with other people, an individual builds a portrait of themselves, rather than the absolute truth. The self-concept is gleaned from others' behavior towards us as well as our desires and evaluation of ourselves. The crux of the paper is to encourage employees to revise the portrait of who they are at their best, and thus paint new possibilities for their future. The idea of social architecture is not new, but RBS theory presents it in an interesting way.

Aligning perspective and perception is sometimes the catalyst to wellbeing, ethical behavior, and the key to developing a sense of personal agency, which can ultimately change perception. The RBS technique is also helpful in evaluating personal injunctive and descriptive norms. Reading the academic paper is suggested, but for the sake of succinctness the basic components of RBS theory consists of four main steps:

Step 1: Collect feedback.
Step 2: Recognize patterns and common themes.
Step 3: Compose your self-portrait.
Step 4: Evaluate and redesign.

To perform Step 1, you must identify and collect feedback from a variety of people, including individuals inside and outside work, family, past and present colleagues, teachers, and also your friends. This will allow you to develop a broader understanding of your true strengths and weaknesses far more than a standard performance evaluation could ever do. Obviously, any participant should be able to offer praise and criticism without being scorned for doing so. Obviously, this step will require more effort than any of the others in the process.

Less time consuming, Step 2 will be trying to recognize patterns and common themes in the information that was collected. What are your behavioral themes for ethics, values, level of curiosity, perseverance, and team participation behavior? Clinically examine the examples of your behavior, but try not to defend those choices. This stage is about looking for patterns. Are you a conformist or an iconoclast? Did you lead the team or follow along? Through your analysis you will certainly find some common themes.

To complete Step 3, you must compose your self-portrait. This is not your interpretation of your behavior or a defensive narrative. With the information gathered, you should be able to write a summarized description of yourself and a composite of who you are from multiple sources. This is meant to be an insightful exercise not a cognitive profile. Writing this summary out fixes the image into your mind and will remind you where the connections are that may have been unrelated before.

Doing Step 4 can be complex. Yet by knowing your true strengths, and not what you imagine them to be, you can make any changes necessary. Think of this like the Scrooge moment when he was allowed to step outside of himself and witness himself in action. Seeing exactly where you have succeeded and failed will help you build on what you are good at and help you make some small changes in the way you work, approach decisions, and build your teams. This kind of meta work will definitely make you a better leader.

There may or may not be a way for an employee to change their organizational culture. However, each person within the group makes up the whole. With this ideal in mind, one person has the power to influence the others, and thus change/impact the culture as a whole. Of course, RBS can be considered academic ideology created by individuals with no actual business experience, but undeniably the concept of self-assessment is necessary in every type of business.

Historically, people have always sought out decisive leaders. Individuals who are aware of their surroundings, and know their own strengths and weaknesses are usually able to attract the talent needed to accomplish whatever objective is necessary. Those with the clearest understanding of external expectations and their ability to meet them are highly valued and coveted assets to any project. On a more pragmatic level, the small details of how you like to work, preferred team composition, and how you spent your time will make a big impact on your effectiveness.

I believe self-reflection is one of the core elements of a great leader. Being accessible, open minded, decisive and accountable are traits all employees look for in a leader, and are also the traits of our chosen heroes. As an employee one may not have control over their organization, but they do have control over how they approach each task. In some cases, knowing how you really are will help you become who you think you are.

How is RBS theory related to good business and decision making? At times, being part of the wrong kind of group, having unresolved communication problems, or not having the time or the specialty to analyze certain details can lead to poor decision making and unintentional adverse consequences. Having an ideal that you strive towards and a realistic assessment of what you need to do to get there will help you get you there faster. Plus, accountability makes every business person better at whatever they do.

As important as it is to reflect on individual ethics theory, it is now time to move onto group ethics analysis. The self-created fictional creation (injunctive) definitely defines individual motivations, while the realistic realm of culture (descriptive) explains group dynamics. The fundamental individual ethical theories like normative theory, social justice models, as well as behavioral and cognitive theory, from the first half of this book should help to add some dimension to case study analysis.

In a business environment, making consensus decisions and managing group analysis is vital and part of everyday operations. Now you can apply the social theory that you learned so far to group theories like compliance, conformity, the halo effect, altruism, leadership, obedience, and reciprocity, which you will discover in the second half of this book. Hopefully, all of the information provided so far proves useful when deconstructing the case studies at the end, and also in real life as well.

REVIEW:

Reflected Best Self (RBS) Theory

Step 1: Collect feedback.

Step 2: Recognize patterns and common themes.

Step 3: Compose your self-portrait.

Step 4: Evaluate and redesign.

GOOD BUSINESS

GROUP   ETHICS

Individual and Group Ethics

Learning, problem solving, and strategy implementation are quite different processes when done in a group setting than when done alone. So obviously, analyzing any ethical dilemma as an individual is different from analyzing it as a group. In a group, individual options entirely change, and even a simple variable like the size of the group can impact the outcome. In fact, in business decisions the group's opinion is often more important than any individual.

The material covered so far has had a strong emphasis on individual choice, which will undoubtedly help you understand how your personal social justice model operates, and hopefully give you insight into those around you. However, engagement within groups is a vital component of business ethics and is sometimes overlooked. Without a doubt the individual analysis will be useful for analyzing groups, but the group concepts in this section will certainly grant you some new perspectives.

Depending on the group dynamics, the size of the group can have an impact on the consensus decision. Some may even argue that the larger the group gets, the value of each individual's contribution is exponentially decreased, which is why strong leaders are needed. Yet is the leader a reflection of the group? Or is the group a reflection of the leader? This is unquestionably a quandary that will result in a neverending debate. Regardless of which paradigm you agree with having insight into how group's operate will undoubtedly enhance your business acumen.

Heterogeneous and homogenous are terms used in the sciences and also in statistics. These key terms relate to the uniformity in a substance or organism, and are also often used to describe the composition of a group or the ideas present. Homogenous groups are uniform in composition or character or may have similar ideas. Heterogeneous groups are distinctly non-uniform (based on certain qualities) and may not share the same ideas.

With most groups, there is usually a homogenous and heterogeneous component/element in both thought and composition. Having groups agree or are similar definitely makes things easier, yet often it is the groups that don't agree or are different that create more depth and breadth to any discussion. In general, too much homogenous thought can lose critical thinking in its conformity. A good quote to remember is a famous comment by Albert Einstein, "When we all think alike, no one thinks very much."

Both a homogenous and a heterogeneous group can suffer from poor communication. Obviously, good communication can serve to enhance a group's intelligence, but knowledge is dissipated with bad communication. Regardless of any strengths or weaknesses in the group, internal communication is useless if it is not objective or cannot be given to the right person at the right time. No matter what kind of group you are participating in, there are a few common paradigms that can affect objectivity.

The halo effect is the common predisposition to admire a person's past work, or hold a favorable opinion based on a previous encounter or prominence. Cognitive embellishments added to past events can also create this delusion. Often in a group, if an "expert" is present, the group can lose individual judgment or precious collaborative information. Non-critical thinking automatic appraisals can regularly affect judgment.

Subject matter divisions within larger groups are great. However, these silos can also create similar problems. Centralized thinking is quite popular in large companies, which often blocks low-level knowledge and experience from finding the decision makers ears so critical information can get lost. If subject matter experts get siloed, the accumulated knowledge is almost useless.

The planning fallacy is a phenomenon in which predictions about how much time will be needed to complete a future task are overly optimistic. In business meetings it is very common for groups to be more optimistic than individuals when estimating the time and resources necessary to complete a task. Anyone involved in business has witnessed this first hand. Psychologists Daniel Kahneman Roger Buehler, Dale Griffin, and Johanna Peetz have clinically proven how this phenomenon is pervasive in groups.

In their pivotal paper "The Psychology of Sunk Cost" Hal R. Arkes and Catherine Blumer discuss how groups are more likely than individuals to escalate their commitment to a course of action that is failing, particularly if members identify strongly with the group. These notions give some clarity as to why companies, states, and even nations often continue with quantitatively doomed projects and plans. This familiar concept is widely known as the sunk cost fallacy.

The sunk cost fallacy leads us to stick with a hopeless project because we have already invested so much into it. Associative blocking or collaborative fixation is where strong ideas block the recollection of other information. Combined with framing effects, which influence decisions according to the semantics of how the options are presented a group can be weaker than an individual. Of course, individual biases will always exist in a group setting, but these impediments can also be countered.

The mental shortcuts (heuristics) that exist in individuals can also exist in a group. Mental heuristics can severely blur objectivity because these shortcuts block certain facts from being noticed and critical data points from being acted upon. Behavioral scientists, Daniel Kahneman and Amos Tversky have identified some common mental shortcuts (heuristics) and biases that have been known to lead individuals and also groups astray.

The availability heuristic leads us to seize on whatever association springs most readily to mind, because it is memorable or we recently experienced it. The representativeness heuristic leads us to believe things or events or people that are similar in one way will be similar in other ways too, when there is no actual connection. The egocentric heuristic is a bias that leads us to exaggerate the extent to which our tastes and preferences are the same as everyone elses.

In a group, there may also be more emotion and social pressure involved in a decision making process than as an individual. Making consensus decisions as a group can also amplify errors, and create a cascading effect stemming simply from following the members who spoke or acted first. Overall, there are many factors/variables that can create a different dynamic or influence a group decision than there are with any individual decision.

Dealing with a business ethics issue on a personal level, rationalization, complacency, stereotyping, and self-delusion exist, but these factors can also corrupt group decisions. Combined with peer pressure, censorship, and the illusion of unanimity, group consensus is that much more difficult. The factors mentioned thus far should help you notice the strengths and weaknesses of the group you are participating in and be mindful of objectivity.

Undoubtedly, understanding group dynamics is important. In high stakes situations, making decisions as an individual can be easier, but as a business person this is not always an option. Knowing your personal social justice model or philosophical predilections may help an individual find a likeminded group, which will definitely help a leader "rally the troops" for an overwhelming endeavor. Yet every good business leader should install mechanisms to get a "no" person to either come up with an alternative, or validate the group's choice by scrutinizing its flaws.

In theory, any group can be helpful or harmful. Critics argue how theoretical concepts are often useless under the pressure of reality. However, these theoretical concepts are only meant to help you analyze a culture or an environment so you can respond effectively. Observing how real groups respond is helpful for both internal and external decision making. Unquestionably, any form of critical thinking enhances ethical decisions. Developing or creating a good group dynamic as a business leader is often difficult, but hopefully defining it now won't be.

REVIEW:

<u>Associative Blocking:</u> When strong ideas block the recollection of other key information.

<u>Framing Effects</u>: Decisions influenced by the semantics of how the options are presented.

GROUP TYPOLOGY:

<u>Homogenous</u>: A group which is uniform in composition or character and may have similar ideas.

<u>Heterogeneous</u>: Distinctly non-uniform in certain qualities and may not share the same ideas.

HEURISTICS:

<u>Availability Heuristic</u>: Leads us to seize on whatever springs most readily to mind, because it is memorable or we recently experienced it.

<u>Representativeness Heuristic</u>: Leads us to believe things or events or people that are similar in one way are similar in other ways, too.

<u>Egocentric Heuristic</u>: A bias which leads us to exaggerate the extent to which our tastes and preferences are typical.

Group Communication

As a businessperson, you will definitely encounter several kinds of groups with a variety of different personalities, so learning some group communication techniques will be essential. Utilizing effective communication techniques can help you assess how an individual fits into the organization and also within the team. Obviously, assembling the "right" individuals is important to a team, but in business this rarely happens. Regardless of the team structure, the ability to communicate will often define its ability.

Intelligence quotient (IQ) is helpful in many circumstances, but can be irrelevant in some problem solving situations. Emotional Quotient (EQ) or emotional intelligence is the ability to identify, assess and control destructive emotions internally and within a group. EQ is what advances careers and builds great teams because in any industry being able to work well with others is a highly coveted skill. Developed EQ can often perceive communication stalemates and reinvigorate blocked progress.

Even with the same culture or team in place, a different leader may have drastically different results than the previous one had with the same conditions present. The

103

reason for this is almost always due to communication flaws. How can any leader ensure all the options, alternatives, risks, and concepts have been covered? Team cohesion, functioning groups, and evolved business units help provide those crucial answers. Assembling a group and then gathering feedback seems simple, but is not easy.

As a business professional, I have participated, led, and studied group dynamics firsthand. By doing so, I have discovered a few simple methods that any group can adopt to solicit participation in solving complex problems. Regardless of the group typology, one of these four basic techniques will inevitably result in some form of unified communication (and also be useful for doing the case studies). These common techniques are brainstorming: dialectical inquiry, nominal group, and the Delphi technique.

Brainstorming is the most popular of these techniques. The unstructured free flow of ideas and concepts in a small group setting can usually facilitate the expansion of concepts. If each person feels comfortable giving an opinion without being evaluated personally, or can add anonymously contradicting ideas, broader problems that may require several iterations can be resolved much quicker. Plus, with a critical dive into a complex problem, a group often bonds. By doing so any problem will have more options and alternatives than any individual can devise alone.

Dialectical inquiry is a very theoretical term for something quite simple. In some groups, the tendency to quickly agree on a universal position can occasionally stifle alternative solutions. Sometimes if the group is divided into two smaller groups where it can debate the advantages and disadvantages of various solutions this planned creative conflict can lead to expanding the discussion. This technique works the same as brainstorming, but sometimes much better.

When separated, different leaders will emerge, and the groups may apply alternative problem solving strategies. This methodology can often help develop a leader's perspective by showing them different solutions to the same scenario, or revealing the exact same decision through two different means. This is also a good way to see how well colleagues are able to work within unfamiliar groups. Overall, this tactic can help test an idea or proposed solution.

The nominal group technique is a more structured method where each member privately writes down a list of ideas of proposed solutions. Then each person can announce one thing from their list, or put them forth anonymously to be compiled to a master list. Typically, no clarification needs to be done, as this is an exercise in getting group members to share their ideas without the worry or fear of criticism.

Often, by removing this reluctance new solutions can be proposed for group debate and iteration. This tactic will help introverts to get their ideas heard amongst extroverts and also provide cover for any individual in the group to share iconoclastic or unpopular ideas. This is similar to a suggestion box, but far more interesting and can even be turned into a light hearted, but constructive game.

The Delphi method was developed by the RAND Corporation. Rand would select individuals in different locations based only on their specific knowledge or expertise of the problem. Like in the nominal group technique, these individuals provide ideas and/or alternative solutions to the decision process. Most every firm has used this method, and have paid subject matter experts (SME) on staff, but never gave it a fancy name like RAND did.

Typically, this method is best done in successive stages, where each member can rank or rate the ideas until the group finally arrives at a consensus on the best course of action. In any group, examining another group's opinions is helpful. Once the list is complete, it is easier to evaluate all of the alternatives and pick the best solution to create the most productive results. Overall, these four simple tactics are not definitive and serve merely as a way to foster group cooperation and leverage the power of a group.

Network theory recognizes communication, formality, proximity, and work flow ties as potential factors in decisions and information flow. At times, these commonalities can cause an inadvertent collusion of opinion. Who talks to whom, who reports to whom, who trusts whom, or who knows whom can change a group dynamic. For innovative initiatives, it can sometimes be good to create groups of strangers.

I have seen good results using these methods. Disbanding social group collusion can both help and hurt the initiative. Working with groups and facilitating discussions will usually help you enhance your EQ and develop leadership skills. A group consensus may not always be in accord with one's own personal values. However, it is this vital disconnect and acceptance that allows groups to work well together.

Considering the material in previous chapters, do you think it would it help you to introduce contrary thinkers into existing groups and teams? Can you spot and identify them now? Based on the philosophy and social justice models discussed thus far would it be beneficial to be in a group of likeminded people or in a group with more debate? It is also important to think about what kind of group or tactics would foster discussion or smother it. Those options are nice, yet deciding on whether to work with a heterogeneous or homogenous group is sometimes not an option.

Obviously, making ethical choices alone is far different from making ethical choices as a group. Whether you are a leader or a member of the group, it is easy to understand how different the dynamics of the decision are when external forces are involved. Take a moment to reflect on what kind of groups you are in, and what kind of results are achieved. How did those experiences affect you? Hopefully, these self-reflective questions can inspire your group communication strategies.

REVIEW:

<u>Ethical Relativism</u>: The idea that ethics are a matter of perspective and relative to the norms of a specific culture.

<u>Heterogeneous</u>: Distinctly non-uniform in certain qualities (thought and group members)

<u>Homogenous</u>: Uniform in composition or character (thought and group members)

<u>Network Theory</u>: Recognizes communication, formality, proximity, and work flow ties as potential factors in decisions and information flow.

Group Brainstorming Methods:

<u>Dialectical Inquiry</u>: Divide the group into two smaller groups which can debate the advantages and disadvantages of various solutions this creative conflict can lead to expanding the discussion.

<u>Nominal Group Technique</u>: Structured method where each member writes down a list of ideas or proposed solutions in writing privately. Then each person can announce one thing from their list, or put them forth anonymously to be compiled to a master list to be discussed as a group.

<u>Delphi Method</u>: Individuals are selected based on their specific knowledge or expertise of the problem and then offer opinions.

Conformity

Do certain activities have their own brand of ethics? In poker, bluffing is part of conforming to the "culture" of the game. Not to do so will lead to failure, and lying is considered appropriate behavior. At times, business people are compelled to misstate the facts. Sometimes conscious misstatements are made, and the concealment or exaggeration of details is sometimes used to persuade customers or vendors. If this is done often enough, does everyone eventually conform?

In a very popular article published in the Harvard Business Review Albert Carr asked, "Is Business Bluffing Ethical?" His concept of deceptology makes the claim that moral standards should be judged on the environment they are in and not for what they are. I believe that comparing business to poker takes the quantitative and qualitative elements out of operations and gives it over to luck, which is quite far from actual strategy. However, peer pressure and the desire to be liked are integral to human existence. So is conformity inevitable?

Alan Page Fiske published "Structures of Social Life" in which he made the claim that people use just four models of social interaction. The four models are: communal sharing (collective responsibility), authority ranking (linear hierarchy), equality matching (restitution in-kind), and market pricing (transactional). According to Fiske, "these models, in varying combinations, organize ideas about social justice, moral judgment, political ideology, religious observance, social conflict, as well as transgression and misfortune."

Several renowned experiments have shown how it is natural for strangers to conform, and not just for selfish, competitive, maximizing, or materialistic reasons. Going against the mainstream is often necessary, but usually it is much more difficult than just remaining within the expected status quo. Why is this psychological theory important to business? Being aware of why people may respond differently than they normally do provides insight into team building. Can social pressure actually make people act differently?

Solomon Asch was a pioneer in social psychology and is best known for longitudinal conformity experiments. His main finding was that group pressure can change opinion or even obvious facts. Certainly, anyone involved in business has witnessed this phenomenon firsthand. Asch's study is quite interesting to read in its entirety, but for the sake of brevity I will summarize it.

A group of liars who knew the outcome of the experiment were placed among smaller subsections of the test group. Each of the participants were shown a card with a line on it and then asked to say which line matched the line on the first card in length. The liars would purposely respond with the wrong answer. The participant could ignore the majority who were blatantly lying or choose for themselves. Asch's aim was to see if the participant would change their answer based on peer pressure.

In this experiment, a considerable percentage of the non-liars changed their correct answer to the incorrect one to appease the group. By doing this, Asch discovered that the bigger the group the more conformity happened within it. This is a fascinating study to read about if you are interested, but for now think of this familiar social pressure as group think. (This term was invented by psychologist Irving Janis).

This kind of conformity also extends to bystander apathy. Social psychologists, Darley and Latane's apathy experiments have shown that when a crime happens or someone is crying out in pain and not one person within the vicinity reacts to stop it, others witnessing it will not react either (even if they know it is wrong). In business, not wanting to speak up about an injustice for fear of being branded as "not a team" player, or purposely ignoring habitual deviations from fixed protocol are examples of this same phenomenon.

By far, the most well-known and most cruel of all social conformity/obedience studies was done by Stanley Milgram. Despite the notoriety of his famous experiment, it revealed a lot about the social power of groups. In fact, this somewhat controversial experiment was inspired by the social debate about questioning totalitarian regimes, and how the participants willfully follow orders to do things that they may not normally partake in.

Milgram's experiment was ingeniously simple. Three individuals were involved: the one running the experiment, the subject/volunteer, and an actor pretending to be a volunteer. Each person had a distinct role. The experimenter was the authoritative role. The teacher role obeyed the orders of the experimenter, while the learner role responded to the stimulus provided by the teacher.

Milgram devised a way to always have the actor "randomly" be picked as the learner, and the volunteer to always be selected as the teacher. Then the teacher and the learner were separated into different rooms. The rules were that each time the learner got an incorrect answer, the teacher was supposed to give them a shock. Before the questioning started, the teacher was given a sample electric shock to experience what the learner would receive during the test. Conveniently, the learner would subtly mention their heart condition.

The teacher would read the word pair question and then read four possible answers. The learner would then press a button to indicate their response. If the answer was incorrect, the teacher would administer a shock to the learner, and for every wrong answer the current would escalate in intensity. Unbeknownst to the teacher, the shocks were not real, and the learner/actor would purposely make

113

mistakes to receive the fake punishment. There were even special sound effects, and the learner would bang on the wall, plead, or complain about their supposed heart condition to further cement the illusion.

When the teachers indicated their desire to stop the experiment, questioned the purpose of what they were doing, or asked to check on the wellbeing of the learner, the experimenter would interrupt them, and tell them to continue. The command would continue, but if the teacher/volunteer wished to stop after four verbal commands, the experiment was halted. Otherwise it was halted after three imaginary 450 volt shocks in succession.

This popular conformity experiment proved one basic thing, most ordinary people were willing to administer what they believed to be painful, even dangerous activity to innocent people if they were told by an authority figure that everyone else was doing the same thing. Strangely enough, and possibly cruel, the authority figure in the experiment was a high school biology teacher who posed as a research scientist.

An even more controversial experiment is Philip Zimbardo's Stanford prison experiment. In a mock prison created in the basement of the Stanford psychology building, half of his volunteers would become prison guards while the remaining ones would become prisoners. The experimenter assumed the role of warden and designed the experiment to induce disorientation, depersonalization, and halt any kind of individualism. In this mock situation, the participants adapted to their roles right away.

The mock prison guards willfully enforced the dictated authoritarian measures, and not only did the prisoners accept the abuse, they even harassed other prisoners who attempted to prevent it. In fact, two of the prisoners quit early and the whole thing was abruptly stopped after only six days. Certain portions of this experiment were actually filmed and excerpts of the footage are available to the public.

What Asch, Milgram, Zimbardo, Darley and Latane proved is what we all intrinsically know, but rarely admit. It is easy to say what you will do in any situation, but this proclamation often changes with the social pressure of a group activity. With the modern explosion of social media and a new array of convenient ways to communicate quickly, group think is even more pervasive. Why is conformity important for business?

Cultural anthropologists who do observation/field work attempt to understand their subject matter through enculturation, which just means adopting the values and behaviors of a specific culture to gain acceptance. Enculturation allows the outsider to observe a culture from an insider's perspective. This process is similar in business for new employees entering a new culture or any businessperson who becomes a new member of an already established social group.

If a leader wishes to launch a new initiative or discover why a problem persists, deconstructing groupthink is a great place to begin. Conformity is also important to analyze as an employee. Business is filled with complex mechanisms and choices. Successful businesses are expected to execute on a strategy where all of its units cooperate, so it is important that all of the various players are "on the same page."

Undoubtedly, both introverts and extroverts seek to belong and create social relationships for themselves. These interactions and connections are the defining points in our lives. Whether we wish to admit it or not, we constantly seek out connections and group approval. In fact, being accepted into certain coveted groups has become a mainstay of modern society. Conformity for social significance or mutual solution is quite common in business and something to be aware of when analyzing group decisions or building teams.

REVIEW:

<u>Fiske's Four Relationship Models:</u>

1. Communal Sharing: Shared suffering and common well-being relationships.

2. Authority Ranking: Linear hierarchy in which subordinates defer, respect, and obey relationships.

3. Equality Matching: Turn-taking and an "eye for an eye" relationship.

4. Market Pricing: Wages, interest, rents, tithes, or cost-benefit analyses relationships.

<u>Bystander Apathy:</u> When crimes happen and not one person within the vicinity reacts to stop it, and an individual immersed in the group who knows what is occurring is wrong, will not either.

Work Design

At any job, absorbing the language, customs, group norms, standards, and public image is typically done within the first year of employment. Over time the mission statement is reiterated enough that it is relatively meaningless. Yet in all forms of anthropology, the analysis of artifacts provides information about the culture of its creator and users. In fact, cultural artifacts (group interaction, habits, shared knowledge, metaphors, and symbols) are often more important than physical objects. How is this relevant to any business activity?

Informed consent is a fancy term used to describe deliberation and free choice. All managers have explicit and implicit assumptions about how to coerce workers into conforming to their requests. Some managers believe workers dislike work and bully them into conformity, while others believe employees like work and strive to create a potentially enjoyable situation. Either style of management is technically an anthropological cultural artifact that shapes the culture of a firm.

Take a moment to answer these questions. Which kind of manager are you? Which kind do you think you are?

118

Which one have you been in the past? Which one have you had? How do you even know which is which? How important is the work environment anyway? Certainly your answers have led you to the same conclusion that I have. The type of manager is crucial to the work environment, because it influences the culture of the firm and the activities performed. Anyone interested in productivity should reflect on how the culture affects output.

From doing observational studies at Hawthorne Works, (a factory outside of Chicago) Henry Landsberger coined the term Hawthorne effect/observer effect. This is where individuals modify an aspect of their behavior in response to being observed. For this commissioned study, the relay assembly firm Hawthorne Works wanted to see if their workers would become more productive in higher or lower levels of light. The thesis of the experiment was to find out if workers are more productive if their needs were met.

In one of the studies, called the "relay assembly experiment" two women were chosen as test subjects. They were allowed to choose four other workers to join their special testing group. Together they worked in a separate room over the course of five years assembling telephone relays. The number finished was the measure of "productivity." A major factor in this study was that they had a supervisor who listened to their needs and at times considered their suggestions.

A few interesting things happened. Considering the

suggested break time length increased productivity, and disregarding it decreased productivity. Shortening the day by thirty minutes increased, and productivity per hour increased, but in aggregate decreased it. Even though adapting to minor changes is not difficult, this concept is still a remarkable study in both individual and group behavior.

Another study conducted by Mayo and Warner was the "bank wiring room" experiment, which studied how payment incentives affected productivity. In this study, 14 men who assembled telephone switching equipment were paid according to their individual productivity. The men formed smaller groups within the larger group and developed informal rules/enforcement mechanisms to control group members and manage bosses. The men performed uniformly wrong to conform to their peer group, thus showing how the social force of their peer group superseded that of management incentives.

It is easy to assume people might be motivated to please the experimenter by changing their behavior to fit interpretation. This assumption is also based on the idea that one performs differently if they know they will be evaluated or measured. Plus, a different setting, social pressure, and researcher bias may also affect outcome. These same elements are quite relevant to most business environments and also employee reviews. How do you evaluate or enhance a work environment?

Two-factor/dual-factor theory also known as Herzberg's motivation-hygiene theory, claims there are certain factors in the workplace that are related to job satisfaction. Maslow's famous paper, "A Theory of Human Motivation" describes safety, belonging, love, esteem, self-actualization and transcendence as the pattern human motivations move through. Frederick Herzberg theorized how job satisfaction and job dissatisfaction act independently of each other.   According to Herzberg, individuals are not content with the satisfaction of lower-order needs at work like minimum salary levels or safe and pleasant working conditions. Rather, individuals look for the gratification of higher-order psychological needs having to do with achievement, recognition, responsibility, advancement, and the nature of the work itself. This is similar to Maslow's theory of how basic needs must be met before the higher needs can be fulfilled.

However, Herzberg added a new dimension to this theory by proposing a two-factor model of motivation. This twist was that the presence of one set of job characteristics or incentives leads to worker satisfaction at work, while another and separate set of job characteristics leads the same worker to dissatisfaction. This theory suggests that to improve job attitudes and productivity, administrators must recognize and attend to both sets of characteristics and not assume an increase in satisfaction leads to decrease in dissatisfaction.

Two-factor theory asserts that motivators and hygiene factors are the most important elements of satisfaction. Motivators are challenging work, recognition, responsibility, or anything that gives positive satisfaction, recognition, achievement, or personal growth. Motivators are intrinsic to the job Hygiene factors are job security, salary, fringe benefits, and work conditions. Hygiene factors provide incentives or are a threat to make someone do something and are extrinsic to the job.

Two-factor theory came from data collected by white collar worker surveys where the respondent was asked to describe periods in their lives of happiness and unhappiness in their jobs. They were asked to describe the sequence of events leading up to the specific moment. Of course, achievement, intrinsic interest in the work, responsibility, and advancement contributed to job satisfaction. Company policy and administrative practices, supervision, interpersonal relationships, working conditions, and salary contributed very little to job satisfaction.

The next step in Herzberg's theory is classifying. Obviously, high hygiene and high motivation is the most ideal situation and is regarded as optimal. High hygiene and low motivation equals a "job as a pay check." With low hygiene and high motivation an employee will have a low salary or low working conditions, but still be driven. Jobs with low hygiene and low motivation are intolerable jobs. This observation is obvious by the demeanor of workers and the scarcity of openings for certain positions.

All jobs have policies, and these can be considered cultural artifacts as well. Analyze the policies in your job both from a managerial and employee standpoint. Do they have just cause and deal with the job performance? Do they have due process and fairness for remedy? Do they have informed consent where the individual has free choice? Lastly, is there comparable pay, with equal rights? These four standards will likely lead to high hygiene and high motivation, and help bring about change when needed.

Almost all of the cultural artifacts present in a firm are dependent on leadership. Is there a difference between managers and leaders? I say yes, and define management as coping with complex changes, shaping activities, and establishing detailed steps for achieving resource allocation targets. I define leadership as developing a vision for the future, and developing constructive strategies to produce that change.

Ideally, management's planning complements leadership's adaptations and creates networks/relationships to accomplish the agenda to ensure their people finish the job. Having high motivators and high hygiene as the standard artifacts of the firm has been proven to enhance group interaction, boost productivity, and create a profitable environment. Informed consent in the right environment can truly make previously unrecognized talent shine.

Why is environment important? Thus far, many examples have been given to show the power of social pressure, and how conformity can influence a group. Armed with this new information, job design should be considered as a component of groupthink. Managing a system and not the people is often the smartest play. With this in mind you will be able to limit cognitive dissonance, increase sustainable productivity, and create a naturally productive culture for any group.

REVIEW:

<u>Two-Factor Theory:</u> Motivators and hygiene factors are the most important elements of satisfaction (Herzberg)

<u>Motivators:</u> Challenging work, recognition, responsibility, and positive satisfaction arising from intrinsic conditions of the job itself, such as recognition, achievement, or personal growth.

<u>Hygiene Factors:</u> Job security, salary, fringe benefits and work conditions.

What is Social Responsibility?

Most business people are aware of what their social responsibility is. Yet how much social responsibility does a business entity need to have? Technically a business is an identity of its own, with agents who do its bidding. Of course, just like people, a company has an idea of its own status. However, this perception is often based on past history, when realistically the present is a far more accurate representation of a firm's true identity. Unfortunately, most firms rarely have the convenience to self-reflect unless a catastrophe forces it to.

Essentially, a business is just a bunch of different parts fit together to form an existence. Even insiders within an organization have differing interpretations what it really is. Again, the concept of injunctive and descriptive norms can be called upon for reflective analysis. However, when a firm operates in one way and states its identity as something else, this corporate cognitive dissonance arouses a flood of negative public sentiment. Who is to blame? The faceless business entity, or one of the various groups/individuals making decisions on the firm's behalf?

Should you analyze the actions of the individuals who are making the decisions? Or analyze their motivations from the perspective of their social group? Or attempt to unravel the business as a whole? Since business decisions are composed of contrasting individuals and groups of diverse thinkers, deconstructing a firm's agency has been a more succinct way to classify an organization's intent and provide a more objective outlook. So what is agency?

Agency can be defined as the motivations of an agent to act on another's behalf when both parties have different interests. The agent is the manager, and the principal is the shareholder and the stakeholders. Agency theory is concerned with resolving problems between principals (shareholders/stakeholders) and agents (company executives). The two main problems agency is meant to address are matching goals and matching risk. Agency problems arise when the desires of the agent and principal are in conflict.

All agents have the ability to operate in their own self-interest rather than in the best interest of the firm because of asymmetric information. Meaning agents have more information than the principal, which at times can be a detriment to this delicate yet symbiotic relationship. Since an agent is able to make decisions on behalf of the principal that impact another person or entity, there exists a dilemma when the agent is motivated to act on their own best interests rather than those of the principal. Moral hazard is the term most often used when describing this type of conflict of interest.

Regardless of the simplicity of this alliance, two conflicting forms of corporate governance have evolved. Both the labor economists (worker) stakeholder mentality stance and the financial economists (investor) shareholder perspective have each been outspoken. Each side has equally valid arguments, and plenty of evidence can be given to describe or justify each stance. In a perfect world, both viewpoints should work together, but they rarely do. Which do you think is better for business?

The answer to this question will entirely depend on if you believe the market is an entity of its own, or if it is the group of people involved in it. This debate is the crux of agency theory arguments and adds a dimension of complexity to business theory. Why is this important? Again, if an individual believes the stakeholder agency is the right one and works for a shareholder agency company, cognitive dissonance might create turmoil.

The shareholder agency exults any investors. This ideal believes the sole purpose of a firm is to make money. Anything in conflict with this is doing a disservice to those who provided the money to fund the firm's operations. Shareholder agency believes that any money devoted to social interest or causes that may not align with the owners/investors is an act of irresponsibility and shows a distraction from the firm's mission. Milton Friedman's article "The Social Responsibility of Business is to Increase its Profits" is considered the foundation of shareholder agency.

Stakeholder agency values both internal and external individuals involved with the company. Internal stakeholders are employees, owners, and managers. External stakeholders are customers, suppliers, government, creditors, society, and also the environment. Primary stakeholders are usually internal, or anyone who might engage in a transaction with the business and secondary stakeholders are considered those affected by the actions of the firm.

As you can see, stakeholder agency has many more factors to consider when developing a strategy and requires a specific kind of manager to operate in this kind of agency. For this reason, stakeholder agency is typically considered to be a more long-term type of thinking. Edward Freeman's "Strategic Management: A Stakeholder Approach" is considered to be the foundation of stakeholder theory.

Does one side of the agency concept need to win while the other loses? Is there a compromise? In Stephen Young's book "Moral Capitalism" he describes a few varieties of successful capitalism that are not a zero sum game. The Japanese interdependent model of "keiretsu" (zaibatsu) is an interesting non-zero sum game style of capitalism that has proven successful. Keiretsu is where, instead of using a bank, a bunch of companies form a group. Then each company in the group borrows money from one another and since they are then interdependent, the companies consult one another on decisions.

In this kind of model, it is hard to argue the shareholder is more important than the stakeholder because essentially they are the same thing. Plus, with a larger interdependent group being involved, a greater spectrum of advice is available. Making everyone a long-term thinking stakeholder rather than a short-term thinking shareholder maintains accountability to equal benefit far more than typical capitalism allows. Despite the advantages of this model, keiretsu is often blamed for creating an incestuous culture of non-inclusiveness and stagnant ideas.

Realistically, stakeholder ideals are a newer concept in the Western world, but the idea of joint venture between equal inhabitants for mutual advantage is not. So regardless of one's ethical model, how could the two conflicting views of agency not be a factor for any individual or group? Economists, Chilosi and Mirella advocate for more employee involvement in corporate governance, and call this increased employee/stakeholder involvement and risk sharing co-determination.

If the employees were shareholders with an employee stock option plan (ESOP), then technically they would be both stakeholders and shareholders. The fragile interdependence of the stakeholders and the shareholders is typically a caustic balancing act. The co-determination ideal is a newer idea in American capitalism, but one that is fundamental in many European companies, and also the basis of Japanese keiretsu.

With ESOP, the leader is accountable to the stakeholder environment, and since everyone has a fiduciary interest they must consider the impact of their actions the company. If an ESOP was standard for all companies, and everyone had input in the decision making process, one of the ethical or justice models would emerge as the driver. If everyone agreed on one course of action, consideration took place and everyone involved knew how decisions would affect them on a personal level.

Without changing anything about American style capitalism the ESOP gives an automatic employee oversight that could easily prevent takeover bids, decrease counter party risk, and create massive company cohesiveness. The ESOP would also be a good way to align the leader's ethics with the individuals they serve. With employee ownership, the oversight principles of responsibility to customers, employees, shareholders, suppliers, competitors, and the community are naturally honored rather than enforced.

Developing an ideal can only be accomplished through responsible and cohesive decision making. Avoiding personal interests from interfering with job duties is the most important capacity of any agent in any form of business. Having a long-term outlook and maintaining accountability are important components of any successful organization. No matter what definition is given to social responsibility or agency, a well-developed long-term strategy is undoubtedly more desirable than a reactive short-term strategy.

REVIEW:

Agency Theory: Matching goals and matching risk between shareholders/stakeholders and principals/ company executives

Agent: Able to make decisions on behalf of, and impact another person or entity.

Principal: The other person or entity who authorizes the agent to work on their behalf.

Principal-agent Problem: (Agency Theory) Since and agent is able to make decisions on behalf of, and impact another person or entity, there is exists a dilemma when the agent is motivated to act on their own best interests rather than those of the principal.

Asymmetrical Information: Since the agent has more and better information than the principal

Agency Cost: The deviation from serving the principal's interests.

Moral Hazard: Occurs when an agent takes more risks than necessary because someone else bears the costs of those risks. Often used to describe a situation where the principal is exploited by the agent serving their own interests rather than those of the principal.

Externality: The effect on a third party by a transaction between two other entities. An externality can be positive or negative.

Stakeholder Agency: Considers the agent's principal to be everyone who interacts with the business

Shareholder Agency: Considers the agent's principal to be only the investor.

Corporate Social Responsibility (CSR)

The economics term externality refers to the effect on a third party by a transaction between two other entities. A home improvement that raises the value of the rest of the neighborhood, and getting immunized and preventing the spread of illness are examples of positive externalities. Property devaluation, disruptive noise, or health issues caused by certain products, are examples of negative externalities. Why does a business person need to know about CSR?

Since all business decisions will have some type of externality, creating programs to address them was an inevitable evolution. In fact, this is why corporate social responsibility (CSR) was created. When CSR was popularized in the sixties, it created controversy. Since then it has become a term used to describe legal and moral responsibility. Public pressure mixed with an employee expectation has pressured modern companies to become more involved in social issues and accept CSR. Although CSR programs are a newer concept in the business world, many firms have intertwined CSR into their mission statement.

Not long ago, CSR was a standalone function with popular public favor initiatives in place. Now, leading companies are learning to integrate CSR into everything they do. Initially CSR placed emphasis on the behavior of the firm. Over time, it expanded to include supplier behavior and the use and disposal of products after they lost value. Now CSR is often used to aid in an organization's mission as well provide a guide for what the company stands for to its consumers. In most modern firms, CSR has permeated all the pieces of the company, to be owned by all functions and staff.

The Caux Round Table (CRT) are ardent supporters of CSR and believe the business community should play an important role in economic and social conditions. The seven CSR concepts that CRT advocates are respecting stakeholders beyond shareholders, showing a contribution to social and economic development, going beyond the letter of the law, respecting rules, responsible globalization, environmental protection, and avoiding illicit activities. These CSR elements are the foundation for business integrity.

Typically, most CSR takes three basic forms: value creation, risk management, or philanthropy. Value creation CSR has a high operational impact by promoting sustainability, competitiveness, and integrating business into the community. Compliance based CSR works to mitigate operational impact, and to support external relationships.

Risk management CSR has a medium operational impact. Philanthropic CSR has a very small impact on operations, but is of significant benefit to the community. Most of the time limited funds are available and are allocated to multiple charities so the impact is diluted.

Coined by John Elkington in 1994, a relatively new concept called the triple bottom line is gaining favor. The triple bottom line is just a catchphrase for accounting for social, environmental, and financial externalities. The Three P's of people, planet, profit or pillars of sustainability have been adopted by some firms as a framework to evaluate their performance in a broader context. Advocates of stakeholder mentality claim CSR is a mechanism of consistency that exists to create a transparent bond between words and action.

Should all businesses have CSR? Shareholders and stakeholders alike can both agree that CSR should not be considered just a program, but more of a consciousness. In the past, social programs were often perceived as a needless capital expenditure. In the more enlightened modern era of knowledge and instantaneous communication, not acknowledging responsibility and ignoring expectation has the perception of being ignorant and archaic.

With our modern, high-speed free flow of information, consumers are more aware of business activities than ever before. In fact, it is becoming the norm for people to "vote with their dollars." Some firms can deny this trend, but this denial can become costly. If a firm operates responsibly and cherishes their place in the community what else do they need to do? How can corporate responsibility even be measured?

The Malcolm Baldrige National Quality Award was established in 1987, and it recognizes businesses for performance excellence. This award is given by the president of the United States, and administered by the Baldrige Performance Excellence Program, and managed by an agency within the U.S. Department of Congress. This award recognizes organizational quality rather than product or service quality and honors Malcolm Baldrige who served as the U.S. Secretary of Commerce from 1981-1987.

The Baldrige Excellence Framework has three parts: improving performance practices, facilitating communications and also guiding planning. The main tenets are delivering value to customers and stakeholders, improving effectiveness capabilities, and organizational learning. There are three main pillars of judgment for the Baldrige Award: governance/stewardship, accountability/communications, and respect. Three awards may be given annually in six different categories, manufacturing, service, small business, education, healthcare, and non-profit.

Overall, there are nine basic principles in the Baldrige assessment: visionary leadership, stakeholder excellence, organizational learning, valuing staff and partners, agility, future focus, societal responsibility, results, and systems perspective. These are certainly standard good practice operating components of successful businesses, yet to what degree they take place is where Baldrige measurements are valuable. All of those factors may seem overwhelming, but each are quantified and calculated.

An outsider's image evaluation is helpful on an individual level, but even more so for an institution. The notion of informed consent is making choices based on accurate information, which is ultimately the highest ideal in any ethical philosophy. Yet CSR is sometimes accused of being fragmented and disconnected from business strategy, and for this reason some corporations do not participate voluntarily. This unspoken reluctance is offset by aggressive social advocates of all kinds that are quite effective at bringing negative public pressure to corporations.

Realistically, no business can solve all of society's problems, and bearing the cost of doing so is absurd and unfeasible. However, if a reluctant firm selects an issue that intersects with their particular business, it will create an economy of scope. An economy of scope is an economic term to describe doing two things for the same cost. Strategic CSR can leverage existing capabilities and also reinforce strategic objectives.

Incontrovertibly, there are several social problems to address. Yet from a business perspective, issues can be classified into three main things: generic social issues, value chain impacts (sourcing and subcontracting issues), and competitive complexities. Generic social issues can be best described as issues that are not affected by the company's operations and have very little effect on their long term strategy.

Regardless of any individual opinions about CSR, throughout history civilizations have always been defined by mutual cooperation. Anthropologically speaking, cultures are measured by the strength of their institutions and organizations. Both social and cultural anthropology concur that all cultures respect value reputation and are willing to invest in it. Social capital cannot be truly measured, but undoubtedly we are all drawn to it.

REVIEW:

<u>Externality:</u> The effect on a third party by a transaction between two other entities. An externality can be positive or negative.

<u>Triple Bottom Line:</u> Accounting for social, environmental, and financial. The "Three P's" of people, planet, profit ("pillars of sustainability")

<u>The Caux Round Table:</u>(CRT) An international organization of senior business executives aiming to promote ethical business practice

<u>Typical forms of CSR:</u>

1. Value Creation

2. Risk Management

3. Philanthropy

Case Analysis Method

How do you know what you know? Is it from experience? Or is it from academic study? The German philosopher Friedrich Nietzsche believed that the central task of philosophy is to teach us who we are. Nietzsche thought there were fundamentally two kinds of knowledge, *erfahrung* and *wissen*. Erfahrung is considered primary knowledge that is learned by doing, and wissen could be classified as secondary information like books, lectures, and television.

Obviously, the human mind is efficient and can process both kinds of information, which is often drawn from when making decisions. By itself, all of the academic theory presented thus far will be helpful for ethical analysis. However, when this theory is put into practice, it becomes a powerful tool. This is why case studies and application is important. When personal experience and past ethical decisions are reflected upon, even more value can be added.

Realistically, everyone has their own method of confronting moral issues. Some people do so by committee while others sojourn with reflective deliberation. When looking at case studies there are several popular approaches. Granted, most case studies revolve around training the individual to program their inductive abilities, but essentially there are two main elements at work.

To review, injunctive analysis is where the observer describes what is perceived to be approved behavior, and descriptive analysis is when the observer describes what actually happened. Some of the moral choice is in the decision and another part is in the justification. If you did the case studies in the beginning, you made some distinctions and rated various choices. If you noted the justification for your decision, it should be interesting to compare this to the ones in your post analysis.

Of course, there are many ways to do case studies, and some ways are better than others. You will likely discover that doing case studies alone might be different than in a group. In school, I learned two helpful ways to analyze case studies in a group setting. The first way was the *CAT methodology* (Case Analysis Template) and the second way was the *5 Ds*. There are many approaches, but I found these to be the most effective for case studies and also in real business cases.

Certainly after the previous chapters, the reader should be able to insert any one of the decision models into each scenario and justify their decision based on those ethical parameters. However, using the CAT and the 5 Ds in a group setting it gives a very interesting perspective and will likely lead to some enlightening conversations. Plus you might discover that being able to justify your decision with structured rationality will allow you to settle on a definitive conclusion. The CAT template is listed below, and will be the first method discussed.

CAT=Case Analysis Template

1. What is the issue?

2. What is the genesis of the problem?

3. What is the challenge?

4. What are the alternatives?

5. Justify the decision.

Within the boundary of the CAT method there are a few *avenues* the group can explore, all of which sometimes lead to a different conclusion and justification than originally expected. "What are the consequences?" This is an interest based discussion based on a consequentialist mindset. "What is the individual's duty to the community?" What are the individual's obligations?" "What is the right thing to do?" These quandaries are all analyses based on a non-consequentialist mindset. These inquiries will definitely broaden the discussion and often help present other points of view.

Avenues

1. Interest based: What are the consequences?

2. Rights based: Does the individual have a duty to the whole community?

3. Duty based: What are the obligations?

143

4. Value based: What is the right thing to do?

As you can see, decision making and ethics is a completely theoretical discipline. So supporting ones conclusions with theoretical concepts is useful for investigating moral domains. Working individually is a self-reflective process done without feedback, whereas working in a group accommodates discovery of how theoretical ethics principals collide yet mutually coexist. When doing any case study it is important to realize there is no one perfect resolution and there will always be objections. Next, I will discuss the Five Ds method.

5 Ds

1. Describe (story of what happened)

2. Discern (issues at hand) Just pick one issue to focus on.

3. Display (options) What are the choices for the one issue you picked?

4. Decide (choice) What is the decision you chose?

5. Defend (justify) Why this is a good decision?

Describe both the main characters and the peripheral ones. Explain what role each participant played and their involvement? In some cases, the characters can be corporations or other institutions, as well as individuals. Facts are open to interpretation, and some may have even been intentionally omitted from the case study that might influence the outcome of the case analysis. Expanding the concept is certainly part of the ethical discovery process.

Since most case studies have several ethical issues, selecting the main issue is relevant for the analysis. *Discern* the principal issue and the collateral ones. There may be a connection between issues either by logical interpretation or by accident. So it is important to separate the various issues to determine the most fundamental one. It may even be helpful to list the moral rights and duties the case involves. Doing so will create discussion within the group and expand on the analysis.

To *display* is to determine what possible actions are open to the various characters in the scenario. Of course there are countless responses and each person in the group may have a unique response. However, specific responses are always better than ambiguous ones. Plus, the group must decipher if the available actions could actually be done based on the information provided. While the group dynamic is going from exploration to consensus, you may notice how some of the earlier social theories will exist during this process.

Decide is entirely focused on isolating and describing the important factual details and ethical issues the case raises. Given the various options available to the characters, what should the various characters do? There will likely be some interpretation about the ambiguous information not provided in the case, but this is where a group decision will be made. Regardless of your individual assessment, the group must somehow come to a resolution as to which response represents the most ethical reaction to the circumstances in question.

If the group is struggling, some of the group communication tactics (brainstorming, dialectical inquiry, nominal group technique, and the Delphi technique) presented earlier may serve to develop the decision further and create more avenues for discussion. In some instances, the case might require a single action, while in other cases it may require several actions. Since the purpose of the case study is to resolve the basic issue, the group may determine there may be more than one action necessary.

The *defend* section will likely be the most difficult. Some justification may have taken place during the decision phase, so the group should be able to support the decision through rational logic. Any of the logical fallacies and assumptions of feelings rather than objective deductions will be transparent at this time. Is the conclusion persuasive when explained? Why is it better than the other choices? Moral knowledge has limitations, and which principles are true or false are always subjective.

Even without absolutism, demonstrating why some arguments are better or worse than others will help support the final conclusion and assist in articulation. By now you may have noticed that some deontological, teleological, or relativistic ideals will have some influence on the case analysis, and may or may not have served as guides. The group resolution might be different than individual preferences, yet many of the theories presented thus far should benefit articulation and compassion for contradicting ideas.

As you can see, the 5 Ds, (describe, discern, display, decide, and defend) are a good method for deconstructing an individual ethical challenge, or can be used to do group work. Whether you decide to use the 5 Ds or the CAT method, both ways will bring perspective. If you read and analyzed the case studies in the beginning, or only just do them now at the end, you may or may not find your opinion has been developed or may have changed entirely.

Why bother with case studies? Being able to come up with a solution and articulate it is a great exercise for any business leader. Doing case studies is also like rehearsing for difficult decision-making situations. This type of exercise can help alleviate pending fear of the unknown, which undoubtedly influences choices. Thus, it is best to consider the case studies like training.

Soldiers are able to function normally amongst gunfire because they have trained for it and expect it. *Warrior ethics* is choosing fight (deliberation) and not flight (reaction). Contemplation is not technically fighting, but making a choice instead of fleeing the decision is often the most difficult part. Learning models and deliberating on situations is no different than training for them to happen. After any kind of training, fear is diminished, decisions are typically less overwhelming, and irrational reactions are less common.

147

REVIEW:

<u>CAT = Case Analysis Template</u>

1. What is the issue?

2. Genesis of the problem?

3. What is the challenge?

4. What are the alternatives?

5. Justify the decision.

<u>5 "D" s</u>

1. Describe (story of what happened)

2. Discern (issues at hand) Just pick one issue to focus on.

3. Display (options) What are the choices for the one issue you picked

4. Decide(choice) What is the decision you chose?

5. Defend (justify) Why this is a good decision?

Post Analysis

First, I would like to say, I hope you enjoyed the material thus far. Before doing these case studies again, reviewing the most well established justice models is necessary. If necessary go back and read the review for Mill and Bentham's utilitarian model, Immanuel Kant's ethic models, Ross' non-consequentialist model, Nozick's libertarian model and Rawls social contract model. Be mindful that some people might be a mixture of more than one model.

Certainly none of these will be better suited than the other for any of the situations, and each case study can be approached using any of these models as a framework. Ethics is subjective and debatable. Yet try to be conscious of how behavior and cognitive theory influences decisions when doing case analysis. It may also be helpful to do your post-analysis using the "Case Analysis Template" (CAT) and/or the "Five Ds."

As I mentioned in the beginning, my goal is for the reader to move from reaction to inquiry, to do reflection versus judgment, to strive for imagination rather than imitation, and to look to create dialogue instead of argument. Ethics and business are often separated, but in many ways these topics are the exact same thing. I hope the material will enhance your decision-making analysis.

<u>Post Analysis:</u>

CASE STUDY 1: "Eminent Domain"

CASE STUDY 2: "Stage Three"

CASE STUDY 3: "Culture Clash"

CASE STUDY 4: "Temporary Fix"

CASE STUDY 5: "Sales Boost"

CASE STUDY 6: "Hot Spot"

CASE STUDY 7: "The Write Off"

CASE STUDY 8: "Free Money"

CASE STUDY 9: "The List"

CASE STUDY 10: "Dumping or Slumping"

CASE STUDY 11: "The Policy"

CASE STUDY 12: "Confidential Information"

CASE STUDY 13: "Foreign Agent"

CASE STUDY 1:
"Eminent Domain"

Two years ago, Michelle Thompson was elected mayor of Martzville. During this time, Collective Manufacturing Inc. (CMI) left the city, and the surrounding neighborhood called the "Grove" fell into decline. Since the majority of the people who lived in this neighborhood had been employed at CMI the area suffered a high unemployment rate that stagnated after the plant closed.

The housing values in the Grove had dropped and this part of the city became a blighted high-crime area. Due to the frequency of petty crimes, Martzville residents avoided the Grove. For years, citizens who lived in other areas constantly complained to Michelle about the neglected homes and the myriad of societal problems that stemmed from this area.

After another dismal report about this neighborhood and another hopeless community meeting in the Grove, Michelle felt defeated and depressed. Later that week, a developer and a representative from Smart Pharmaceuticals Corporation (SPC) set up a meeting to discuss moving their corporate headquarters to Martzville. During this meeting, several sites were proposed, but the developer and SPC were only interested in the old CMI site in the Grove area.

Michelle left this meeting ecstatic, but still reflected on the disappointing community meeting earlier that day in the Grove. When she got back to her office, she received a call from the developer's attorney. During this call, the attorney reviewed the developer's plans. It was not until this point that Michelle realized the old CMI site was definitely not big enough for the proposed project.

As the attorney spoke about "eminent domain" laws, Michelle knew he was right, and there was no other option. It was true that the US Constitution allowed the government to seize land for "public use" as long as there is "fair compensation." Plus, Michelle was acutely aware of how the property values in the Grove had sharply fallen, and that many of the residents had abandoned their homes and moved to a new city when CMI left.

The SPC headquarters deal would be an opportunity for Martzville to revitalize this dysfunctional area, and bring in new high earning jobs and employees. The new corporate headquarters would add much needed tax revenue and completely change the Grove from a neglected and useless area of the city to a coveted part of Martzville. As the attorney spoke about what was required, Michelle thought over the consequences of such an action.

Deep down she knew the SPC development was exactly what Martzville needed. However, the economically challenged residents in this area would likely receive far less for their property than what they paid for it. Since many of the residents in the Grove would not be able to afford a new house, many of them could be left homeless or even worse.

She took a deep breath and then asked the fast talking attorney to call her back in two days. After she hung up, she stared out of the window and thought over what would happen next. She knew SPC had other cities in mind as well, and the attorney had made it very clear that the eminent domain option was the only way SPC would come to Martzville. Should she move forward with the plan, or deny the project? Why or why not?

CASE STUDY 2:
"Stage Three"

A talented chemical engineer, Puja Wharton left her Fortune 500 job to start her own biotech business. Holding the patent to a new kind of drug, she felt confident her invention would be successful in the market place. After only being in business for six months, her managers were showing her preorders. In fact, the preorders were far more than her small firm could handle at their current capacity.

Even with the patent and a flood of pre-orders, her team still needed to still go through stage three testing. Only after this stage was complete could they get approval from regulators to go to market. This test was by far the most important, and Puja knew that if the drug did not pass, the remaining capital of the firm was not enough to proceed with another round of expensive testing.

A surplus of preorders still continued to flood in as Puja and her team worked day and night to perfect the formula. On the day of the test, the drug failed due to the nasty side effects. Unfortunately, her customer's orders were dependent on approval and the news of the failure would be confidential

155

until the follow-up test.

Puja and her team felt confident that the drug just needed one more small adjustment to pass the follow up. However, it was unlikely that she could afford to pay for another expensive round of testing. If she borrowed the money or got a new investor, there was a chance that the news of the stage three testing failure would go public.

Undoubtedly, her drug would help millions of people if it could go to market. Daily, her managers showed her how eager her customers were about buying the drug, and had even showed her a recent report of a very similar drug coming to market soon. Then they shared the dire financial reports and showed her on the calendar exactly when they would need to file for bankruptcy.

With diminishing capital, her managers presented her with two options. Then they left her alone to decide between the option of selling the company and the patent to a large corporation for two million dollars, or going to Russia to test.

Going to Russia to test would be cheaper and due to corruption her manager assured her the drug would be approved there. After it went to market her firm would make over fifty-million dollars. This money would buy her time to tweak the formula and possibly alleviate some of the unstable side effects. Which option should Puja choose and why?

CASE STUDY 3:
"Culture Clash"

Xavier Rhodes, a poor kid from a working class family worked really hard as an intern and then got his first job on Wall Street. Working as a broker at a major firm was always his dream job, but he still hoped to move up the corporate ladder. Despite his connections from school and the extra hours he put in to get an established pipeline of clients he was continually passed over for promotion.

His expensive Ivy League education had opened some doors for him, but not enough of them to pay off any of his crushing student debt. It was also painful for him to watch the firm that he worked for give out lavish rewards for sales goals, which he rarely ever met. Typically, Xavier skipped lunch to work with clients, but after being prodded by some of his college friends, he finally decided to attend a lunch get-together.

The lunch meeting was cordial, but Xavier grew tired of how most of his friends bragged about their new promotions and higher salaries. He looked around the room and then took a deep breath. Seated next to him was Jack Bilsten. Jack worked at a competing firm across town, but was also an acquaintance of Richard Halstrom, Xavier's boss.

After a few cocktails, Jack pulled Xavier aside and asked Xavier if he would show him the premarket and closing orders of his biggest clients before placing them. If he did so, Jack would route some big orders to him, which would result in a higher commission. Xavier knew that included with the higher commission he would receive high priced season tickets, and two roundtrip plane tickets anywhere in the world. Plus, Jack also promised to help him get promoted.

When the lunch meeting concluded, Xavier and his friends remained, but Jack left and went back to his office. Listening to their boisterous conversation, Xavier discovered how most of them had shared their client's orders with Jack before they placed them. Each of them freely admitted that they now enjoyed a higher salary, and had also gained a higher position in their firms from doing so.

Despite this activity being highly illegal, Xavier was certain no one would ever find out he was sharing the orders with Jack. The majority of his clients were big enough that skimming a few dollars off of the order by letting Jack front-run his own in front of it would not matter. He had never considered this scheme before, but since most of his friends were already doing this, Xavier pondered if this kind of activity was just part of the industry.

On his way to work the next morning, Xavier's phone rang repeatedly, but he did not answer it until the third call. On the other end was Jack. Eager to hear whether Xavier would commit to the plot, Jack sounded impatient. Claiming that he was in transit, Xavier diverted answering the question by saying he would call back in ten minutes. What should Xavier do and why?

CASE STUDY 4:
"Temporary Fix"

Yang Xiong was tired of working as an auditor in a major firm, but he still made an appointment to complete the last test of his CPA certification in three weeks. At his weekly golf outing with his best friend Diego, Yang shared his disgust for the firm he was currently employed at. Diego listened through the long discourse and then mentioned how he was in need of a new CFO.

Yang knew his skills would fit the role of CFO and since he and Diego had known each other since the fifth grade, he immediately offered his services. Without a moment of hesitation, Diego offered him the job. In the span of two breaths, Yang accepted and then called his boss right then and resigned. Yang was as excited as he was intimidated to get to look at the books of Diego's giant firm, and he could not wait to start.

On his first day, Yang met his new staff and got even more excited when he moved into his new top floor office with a picturesque view and posh interior. With a spare moment, he checked his brokerage account. His eyes were instantly drawn to the value of the stock options he had been granted for his new CFO position. When he realized the number was real, his jaw literally dropped. The options granted to him were more than he had gotten in ten years of work as an auditor.

Sitting down at his lavish desk he vigorously pored over the books. Upon his first analysis, some things did not appear right. After further inspection, he noticed several small details did not match, so he ordered more material to be sent to his office, and then he toured the manufacturing facility, the warehouse, and then the document storage room.

After returning to his office and doing more forensic analysis he discovered several entries that were made to mask losses. From there he discovered a trail of entries that indicated Generally Accepted Accounting Principles (GAAP) were being ignored. Digging in further, he realized the manipulation of the books was done primarily as a mechanism to prop up the stock price.

Leaning back in his cozy chair, he stared out at the impressive view and deliberated his options. The entries were layered so cleverly that only one of his former colleagues in all of the auditing firms he had worked at would be able to notice them. When the phone rang he ignored it and went to meet Diego for their usual game of golf.

On the second hole, Yang mentioned some of the accounting irregularities. Diego just dismissed them as only temporary entries kept in place until the firm's sales stabilized. On the third hole, Yang asked a few more questions. When confronted, Diego admitted how these kinds of entries had been ongoing, and had already passed through multiple audits undetected. On the way to the fourth hole, Diego requested that Yang relax and conform until sales got better. What should Yang do and why?

CASE STUDY 5:
"Sales Boost"

Two years ago, Vihan Turner, a tenured manager, was promoted to manage a failing product line, and his company moved him across the country. Despite having to sell his beloved home and relocate, he viewed the promotion as an opportunity, and was eager to make the move. He and his wife both agreed that the salary increase and mild weather would increase their family's quality of life.

Over the last couple of years, his wife and children thrived in the community and were convinced that the new job was an improvement to the quality of their lives. Best of all, Vihan's youngest child was able to finally receive proper medical attention for her disability and see an expensive specialist located in the area.

Everything went well with the new job except each day Vihan was faced with the same lagging sales problem as the previous manager. Throughout his tenure he struggled to fix this pervasive problem, and tried several tactics, but nothing worked. Since Vihan's job depended on the success of the product line, every day he sought out options for a remedy.

After receiving another stern warning from the corporate office, Vihan began to aggressively interview candidates for several recently vacated sales positions. He hoped to find an all-star sales guru who would revive sales and inspire his existing team. Due to his age, he felt that if he were fired, finding a comparable position would be hard. Not only would he need to downsize, his child's medical condition would likely worsen without company subsidized health care.

When the last candidate, Amir Madani opened his briefcase he winked as he put a business card on the table. With a quick glance he noticed a recognizable government official's name on it. Before he could inquire, Sam proposed a scheme that would likely increase sales. Vihan was acutely aware of how certain markets were off limits due to sanctions, yet Amir promised he could get access to them through bribery. Vihan knew the untapped market had enough demand to solve his sales problems and appease the corporate office.

While Amir explained how his bribery scheme would transpire, Vihan listened and pondered. Then Amir proposed that Vihan hire him at an entry level salary, but give him exclusive access to all of the commissions derived from the sales in the untapped market. Everyone believed the ban was unjust and limited the freedom of the individuals in the region. It was only a matter of time before the sanctions were eventually lifted.

Vihan knew how the off-limits region needed his company's product, and how badly Amir needed a job. Vihan also knew that the corporate office would relax and let him keep his job and health benefits if he increased sales. Although he would have to set up a reoccurring bribe to maintain access to the off limit country, he would definitely not get fired. Should Vihan hire Amir and go through with plan? If so why? If not why? What should Vihan do?

CASE STUDY 6:
"Hot Spot"

As a new restaurant owner, Jon struggled. In fact, business was so bad, and his debt was so high that he would have to sell his house to fund the failed enterprise for a few more months, or just consider closing. When Stan, an experienced former restauranteur was hired as head chef, Jon's faith was reinvigorated as he was inspired by Stan.

Over the next few weeks, Stan's impact was obvious. The culture of the restaurant had completely changed, business had picked up and there was clearly a new local buzz about the restaurant. Things were happening fast, and revenue was growing just as quickly. In just a few months, Jon was nearly out of the red, and the restaurant was packed every single week.

While Jon pondered how he might promote Stan, he overheard two customers talking about one of his competitors, the Grotto. Apparently, the chef at the Grotto had hepatitis, and if word got out of this it would negatively affected the business. Then later that day, Stan's ex-wife came in and pulled Jon aside.

In this private meeting she revealed how Stan had

contracted hepatitis, and she explained how his affliction was the catalyst for him closing his own successful restaurant. Whether this was true or false, this was a serious accusation. Before the start of Stan's shift, Jon had originally planned to award him the promotion, but now he was pensive.

Rather than meeting privately with Stan, Jon refrained and instead he went for a walk. Jon was acutely aware of how Stan was the catalyst to his new found success and was the savior of his restaurant. If he were not there, it would definitely be a morale blow to the staff, and since many customers asked for him, it would be difficult to explain why he was not there.

Jon thought about how he would feel if he and Stan were in opposite positions. Jon felt asking Stan the status of his health, and inquiring about his relationship with his ex-wife, would be awkward, and also highly inappropriate. Stan was a great chef, but he was temperamental, and might quit if he was confronted. After a long walk, Jon reflected as he made his way back to the restaurant.

When Jon realized how Stan had recently taken several sick days, this made him even more nervous. Plus, if Stan had hepatitis he was definitely not eligible to work in Jon's restaurant, and may spread it to his staff and patrons. A block away from the restaurant, Jon stopped and stared up at the glowing sign and exhaled deeply. What should Jon do, and why?

CASE STUDY 7:
"Write Off"

At Steelhammer Utilities, Hazel McNelly had worked her way up from the bottom. Now as a vice president she had her own cost center and was finally in a position to award contracts. She was well respected in the industry and had over ten years of experience with various vendors. Hazel was regarded so highly that she was recently awarded a new office twice the size of her old one.

Hazel was about ten years away from retiring and had built up a nice retirement portfolio, but it was still not enough to allow her to support her current lifestyle. On the side, she had invested all of her meager bonuses for the last five years into Bell Weather (BW), a local company with a listed stock on a public exchange. She felt BW was a great company and appeared to be far undervalued.

On Friday, she received a call from BW requesting a meeting. Typically she would not consider small unproven companies like this, but she thought this opportunity might help BW to achieve greatness. When asked to consider rewarding them a major contract, she left the meeting with the financials in hand.

166

As an investor in BW, she had seen their public financials before. Even with an initial glance, she knew there was something different about the documents that she'd been given. After a brief examination, she saw no ability for them to honor the agreement and no feasible way for her firm to use the materials in full capacity. In fact, if the financials they had provided were accurate, BW had become insolvent.

Hazel knew there was potential for the news media to perceive this contract as good news, and since she had a big portion of her retirement portfolio invested in BW, she could probably sell her stock at a decent gain to exit the position. She also knew that after the new financials she had just reviewed became public, BW stock would tank. Either way, it was imperative that she immediately unwind her current position in BW before she was wiped out.

Hazel paced around her spacious office, and deliberated. Even if she awarded the contract and BW could not deliver on it, her successful firm could easily write the uncollectible off as a loss, and there were plenty of other vendors she could get for the job. Since she was a trusted expert at her company and also in her industry, she was certain she would not lose her job. While she deliberated, her contact at BW sent her an email including improved financials, which included the revenue from the pending contract. What should Hazel do and why?

<u>CASE STUDY 8</u>:
"Free Money"

After working for Pressfield Inc. for several years, Rick Colland finally got to be the manager of the sales division. His brother Jayden also worked at the company. Both of the men were excited to discuss this wonderful news. After work, they went out and celebrated the promotion. At the first upscale bar, Jayden was overly generous and picked up the expensive tab.

Reflecting now, Rick felt apprehensive about how Jayden had been buying him lavish lunches, but he had never questioned it. They had so much fun that he ignored his suspicion on this occasion as well. After a night out, Rick drove Jayden home and they reminisced about old times. Once they arrived, Jayden reached into his pocket and handed his brother an expensive cell phone as a congratulatory gift for his new promotion.

The next day, Rick began his day by reviewing the budgets with the controller. When questioned about high expenses Rick asked for time to do the proper research and then explain his findings. Looking over the expense accounts and analyzing the data, he noticed his brother Jayden had the most discrepancies.

Upon further research, he discovered Jayden was buying electronics with the company expense account and then likely reselling them at a profit. When searching through the evidence he was careful and unbiased, but everything pointed to this conclusion. The evidence was undeniable.

Later that week, Rick was sent out of town for an important meeting with a vendor, and on the grueling flight home he pondered about what he should do. When he returned, Rick confronted his brother Jayden. When pressed on the matter, Jayden admitted to buying appliances with his expense account to resell them, and justified his actions.

Considering Rick knew how Jayden would eventually get caught, and it would not be long before his scheme was detected, he pleaded for Jayden to confess. Ignoring his plea, and then adding a twist, Jayden mentioned he had used Rick's password to secretly sign off on the purchases. In shock about what he had just heard, Rick froze up. What should Rick do and why?

CASE STUDY 9:
"The List"

Jim and Tiffany worked as account managers at a local insurance company for three years. The fourth year, they began dating and soon after got married. It has now been five years since they started at the company, and they still work together. Over the span of five years, Jim and Tiffany built a profitable client list and had made a wonderful life together. Nearly everything was perfect, except Larry, their tyrannical overbearing manager.

Midweek, Jim had another big argument with Larry, which led to Jim slamming the door of his office in Larry's face. After a quick phone call, Jim was hired on the spot by a rival company into the same position. His new employer was openly interested in Jim bringing all of his clients with him. Despite this request, Jim reflected on the generous offer.

Guaranteed a big promotion if he could convert fifty percent of his old clients to his new firm, Jim analyzed the coveted client list that he had virtually memorized. If he were to pitch these clients he was sure they would convert and bring their business to his new firm. The problem was he and his wife Tiffany built the client list together.

Realizing his dilemma, Jim decided to petition his new boss to hire Tiffany. His new boss agreed, but unfortunately she did not want to change jobs. When Jim told her he had been in secret negotiations with their best clients, and had already convinced some of them to go to the rival firm, she got visibly upset and nearly left the room.

When she paused to mention how this would probably affect her bonus and could cause her to lose her job, she grew even more agitated. By now, she was so upset that she was shaking, which got worse as she shared how she thought Jim had over reacted to Larry's behavior. Jim was silent as Tiffany admitted her disappointment about his new job at the competing firm. After a big argument, she left angry.

Tiffany had not come home for three days, and Jim was beyond worried. Despite this, his new boss gave Jim an ultimatum. He must convert his previous firm's clients to his new firm, or else he could not work there. Barely paying attention, Jim's mind was on Tiffany.

Jim took the long way home and deliberated over his dilemma. When he got home, Tiffany was there. Overcome with emotion, she admitted her recent marital infidelity to him. After squabbling over who was at fault, they decided to resolve their animosity and discuss their mutual problem.

Without a resolution, Jim and Tiffany went to work the next day. Right when Jim arrived, his boss stormed into his office and pressed him to deliver the client list. Right from the beginning, Jim began receiving phone messages and emails from his old clients to inquire about his services, but he was purposely slow to respond.

Jim knew if he did not deliver the client list as expected, he would be demoted or may even lose his job. Considering how tenuous his relationship with his wife was and how Larry would probably not allow him to go back to his old job, he knew he had to make a decision. Jim left the office early and took the longest possible route home. What should Jim do and why?

CASE STUDY 10:
"Dumping or Slumping"

Before he took a sabbatical and invented the wonder drug Fabion, Elias Robowski had worked in many labs over the years. After his big discovery, he created Robco. Over the span of two years, he created other drugs, but his revolutionary drug Fabion was still by far the biggest seller. The success of this product and his company were life changing for both Elias and his family.

With Robco experiencing such high demand for Fabion, Elias planned to expand production. To confirm his strategy, he hired a market research company to provide him with an accurate market forecast. Just like he expected, Elias received a positive outlook, and every source of data confirmed continued demand. With this news, Elias ordered his factory to produce twice the usual amount of the Fabion.

While counting the increased inventory of Fabion, he was pulled aside by his operations manager. In the private meeting, his manager shared the recent notice from the Consumer Product Safety Commission (CPSC). Regretfully, the operations manager informed Elias about how the CPSC had just prohibited the sale of Fabion. After hearing this news, Elias was livid that this message was not shared with him before he ordered the increase in production.

Once Elias calmed down, the operations manager explained a loophole in the CPSC ban. Other countries' medical communities sometimes have different conclusions regarding safety that differed from the conclusions reached by the U.S. medical community and the Food and Drug Administration. Just because a manufacturer can no longer sell the banned product in America, the product could still be sold in other countries that have not prohibited its sale.

He further explained that some foreign researchers had conducted the same studies on Fabion, but they concluded that only stronger warning labels were needed. His manager recommended that Robco "dump" the recalled product and inventory surplus in other countries or they would need to take a write-off that would damage earnings, stock prices, and employment stability. Since the inventory of Fabion was high, Elias knew that chaos would follow a product recall.

Considering how there were now some serious safety concerns about Fabion, and Robco was holding a substantial inventory of a product that has been outlawed in the U.S. what should Elias do? Dump the recalled product and excess inventory in other countries that did not ban its sale? Or should he direct his operations manager to take the write-off, which would hurt the company's earnings for the next two years, and likely result in layoffs?

CASE STUDY 11:
"The Policy"

A year ago Pam Ingbretson the human resource director for Triton Inc. hired her nephew. Then a year later she hired her daughter Ellen. HR had a policy that an employee cannot take off more than three personal days a month, and cannot be late more than twice. I was an HR policy to give out points for each time an employee was late or tardy. If an employee got too many points they were terminated. However, this policy was not always followed.

Throughout the year, Pam's daughter Ellen was absent and late on several occasions. Despite Ellen's points getting quite high, she continued to be late, as well as take unapproved personal days whenever she wanted to. Her constant absences and blatant disregard for policy were well known amongst her peers and affected both employee morale and production.

When the holiday season finally arrived, Pam was excited to celebrate her favorite time of year. When Pam logged in to her workstation, she got an urgent automated email reminder. Apparently an employee had exceeded their personal points threshold for the third time and severe action needed to be taken. The name at the top of the notification was her daughter Ellen Ingbretson.

When Pam saw the accumulated points at the bottom, she immediately went into Ellen's personnel file. Then she inspected the attendance sheet for a while before she keyed down to the threshold number at the bottom. She knew she had the authority to make Ellen's threshold higher or just adjust her points to be under the threshold. Her other option was to follow through with the current policy and terminate her daughter.

Pam stared over at the picture on her desk of Ellen's three children. As a single mother herself she knew exactly how challenging it was to get three children off to school and then get to work on time. There were others in the firm who had a similar burden, but her daughter's plight was unique. Not only did she have three kids to tend to, Pam was fully aware of her daughter's pending bankruptcy filing because she had recently borrowed her enough to pay her mortgage.

The cursor on her screen blinked while Pam considered her options again. If she made Ellen's threshold higher, she would have to do the same for everyone and then send out an announcement that the threshold had been universally raised. If she adjusted Ellen's points to be under the threshold, this may get flagged on the next corporate audit, which would affect her job.

She looked away from the screen as she reflected. If she followed through with company policy and terminated her daughter, she knew Ellen would have a difficult time finding new employment and her financial troubles might further compound. This decision would also have an impact on the upcoming holiday season. What should Pam do and why?

176

CASE STUDY 12:
"Confidential Information"

Candace had been a manager at Safeco for two years. She enjoyed her job and looked forward to going to work each day. She respected all of the employees in her store because all of her direct reports had been her coworkers before her promotion. However, over time they grew apart, and due to her new position she was not able to attend social events like she had before. Despite this fact she still felt a kinship and was grateful for the group solidarity and teamwork that existed in her store.

Recently, her district manager met with her to discuss the inventory problem in her store. Inventory shrinkage is common in retail, but her store had much higher shrinkage than the typical industry standard, or any other store in the corporate footprint. Candace was aware of this problem, but she had not realized her store had the biggest problem in comparison to others. Before she left the meeting she promised to put remediation methods in place.

When she got back to the store, she put out an ad to hire some security guards as well as some secret shoppers.

After three weeks, she did an inventory count and discovered that nothing had changed. The shrinkage problem still existed, and was now even worse. Her next remedy was to install security cameras. After a few weeks, she eagerly reviewed the surveillance.

After doing so, Candace discovered her employees were not stealing, but instead were doing other things. Two of them were having a very physical love affair while on the clock, another was engaging in a fraudulent food stamps scam, and another was leaving early and having a coworker punch out for them later. She exhaled deeply, and then examined the records in search of the source of the inventory problem.

While Candace was deliberating a new approach to the problem, she inadvertently discovered how the vendors were shorting her on her orders. She never told the employees they were being filmed and recorded. Since the reason for cameras was to decipher the cause of the inventory shrinkage, she knew she could get rid of the cameras, yet her boss was hesitant to do so. She also had to deal with the issues she witnessed on the surveillance footage. How should Candace approach this with her employees and with her district manager? Should she inform the district manager?

CASE STUDY 13:
"Foreign Agent"

As a youth, Abdi moved to America from Kenya. Over the years he worked several menial jobs simultaneously while he attended school. After graduating with honors, he got a job at LeVain Oil Corporation. When he discovered LeVain needed a representative in Kenya, he jumped at the chance to represent the firm in Kenya.

After he'd met most of the top level executives at the firm, each of them raved about how impressed they were with Abdi's intelligent answers and his stunning business acumen. The vice president of the division even sent a personal note to Abdi expressing his confidence in Abdi's ability to expand their business in Kenya. Even though he got a significant pay raise, Abdi was more excited about moving back home than the extra pay.

After a few months, LeVain did their standard expense audit, and quickly discovered how Abdi had rented an apartment in his old neighborhood, a well-known slum in Nairobi. Yet on his subsidized rent form, a different address in a rich neighborhood was listed. It appeared to the audit group that Abdi was expensing $2000 a month for somewhere he did not live. After reviewing the evidence again, the lead auditor brought this discrepancy to management. After learning of this, all of the managers universally agreed to send a representative to find out more about this issue.

When the representative confronted Abdi about this, he did not hide what he did. He claimed that since most of the other executives expensed at least $2000 a month, he thought he should be allowed to do so as well. He also mentioned how he would be considered a target and be vulnerable to thieves if he actually lived in the more expensive place he listed on the form. The LeVain representative's suspicion was noticeable, so Abdi continued.

He further justified this secondary residence by saying how the extra money from the $2000 allotment compared to what he spent for the apartment in his old neighborhood was enough to send his nieces and nephews to school. When pressed further, he said that by being a successful executive, paying for his family's school was expected of him. When the representative returned and shared this information with the managers, a decision needed to be made. What should the LeVain managers do about this, and why?

Before you go...

Thanks for reading. I hope you've enjoyed this book as much as I loved writing it. I appreciate every one of you for taking time out of your day or evening to read this. If you have an extra second, **I would love to hear what you think about it**. Please leave a comment on Amazon. To check out my other books, visit my Amazon page.

If you are interested in reading more about philosophy and ethics you should definitely check out these thought provoking books and papers. All of which are FREE at most local libraries. This list is not ranked.

REFLECTIVE BOOKS AND PAPERS

"Nicomacean Ethics" by Aristotle

"A Study in Moral Theory" by Alasdair MacIntyre

"The Republic" by Plato

"The Richest Man in Babylon" by George S Clason

"The Art of Happiness" by the 14th Dalai Lama

"Groundwork of the Metphysics of Morals" by Immanuel Kant

"The Moral Landscape: How Science Can Determine Human Values" by Sam Harris

GOOD BUSINESS

"*Introducing Lacan*" by Darian Leader

"*Ethics 101: What Every Leader Needs to Know (101 Secrets)*" by John C. Maxwell

"*Papers on Metapsychology*" by Sigmund Freud

"*Beyond Good and Evil*" by Friedrich Neitzsche

"*Utilitarianism*" by John Stuart Mill

"*Meditations*" by Marcus Aurelius

"*How to Read Lacan*" by Slavoj Zizek

"*Acres of Diamonds*" by Russel H. Conwell

"*The Power of Positive Thinking*" by Dr. Norman Peale

"*The Wisdom of Crowds: Why the Many Are Smarter Than the Few and "How Collective Wisdom Shapes Business, Economies, Societies and Nations*" by James Surowieki

"*How Good People Make Tough Choices*" by Rishworth M. Kidder

Ecrits, by Jacques Lacan

Work and the Nature of Man, by Frederick Herzberg

The Lucifer Affect: Understanding How Good People Turn Evil, by Philip Zimbardo

Management and Morale, by Fritz Roethlisberger

Outliers, by Malcolm Gladwell

Is Business Bluffing Ethical, by Albert Carr

Edward Freeman's *"Strategic Management: A Stakeholder Approach"*

Alan Page Fiske's *"Structures of Social Life"*

Applied Intelligence, by Robert Sternberg

The Theory of Multiple Intelligences, by Howard Gardner

The Social Responsibility of Business is to Increase its Profits, by Milton Friedman's

The Motivation to Work, by Frederick Herzberg

Lincoln on Leadership, by Donald T. Phillips

Obedience to Authority: An Experimental View, by Stanley Milgram

A Theory of Human Motivation, by Abraham Maslow

The Individual in a Social World: Essays and Experiments, by Stanley

"Self-Discrepancy: A Theory Relating Self and Affect" Tory Higgins

Changing Minds, by Howard Gardner

Moral Capitalism, by Stephen Young

The Sublime Object of Ideology, by Slavoj Zizek.

Toward a Psychology of Being, by Abraham Maslow

The Nature of Intelligence, by Louis L. Thurstone

Multiple Factor Analysis, by Louis L. Thurstone

The Philosophy of Moral Development: Moral Stages and the Idea of Justice, by Lawrence Kohlberg

A Theory of Human Motivation, by Abraham Maslow

Key Terminology:

<u>Agency</u>: The motivations of an agent to act on another's behalf when both parties have different interests.

<u>Agency Theory</u>: Concerned with resolving problems between principals (shareholders/stakeholders) and agents (company executives).

<u>Artifacts</u>: Provides information about the culture of its creator and users. (cultural artifacts are group interaction, habits, shared knowledge, metaphors, and symbols)

<u>Associative Blocking</u>: When strong ideas block the recollection of other key information.

<u>Attended Stimulus</u>: The specific objects in the environment that attention gets focused on.

<u>Asymmetric Information</u>: Agents usually have more information than the principal, which at times can be a detriment to this delicate yet symbiotic relationship.

<u>Behaviorism</u>: Is the study of behavior for the purpose of identifying its determinants and analyzing the patterns triggered by a stimulus.

<u>Bystander Apathy</u>: When crimes happen and not one person within the vicinity reacts to stop it, and an individual immersed in the group who knows what is occurring is wrong, will not either.

<u>Categorical Imperative</u>: An absolute unconditional requirement that must be obeyed in all circumstances and is justified as an end in itself.

<u>Co-Determination</u>: Employee involvement in corporate governance, and increased employee/stakeholder involvement and risk sharing.

<u>Cognitive Dissonance</u>: Mental stress or discomfort experienced by an individual who holds two or more contradictory beliefs, ideas, or values at the same time, or is confronted with new information that conflicts with existing beliefs, ideas, or values.

<u>Cognitive Theory</u>: explores intelligence, personality, state of mind and perception with a focus on individual reasoning.

<u>Competing Rights</u>: Two ideas are both sound, but different.

<u>Corporate Social Responsibility (CSR)</u>: A term used to describe legal and moral responsibility. CSR programs have been intertwined into some firm's mission statement. (Three basic forms: value creation, risk management, or philanthropy).

<u>Deontological Theories</u>: Duty based ethics, non-consequentialist motivations.

<u>Descriptive Norms</u>: What you actually did and how you behaved in the situation.

Dissonance Reduction: Done to bring cognitions and actions in line with one another.

Due Process: Fair treatment through procedural administration where both sides have a chance to present evidence and make claims. Due process typically has fairness and a remedy.

Emotional Quotient (EQ): or emotional intelligence is the ability to identify, assess and control destructive emotions internally and within a group. (See erfahrung)

Environmental Stimulus: Far too complex to consume all at once, but this aspect is a starting point for cultural awareness.

Epicureanism: Physical in nature, and believed that happiness in its highest form was achieved through the removal of physical pain and mental anxiety through indulging in physical pleasure. Epicureans were spontaneous and attuned to their awareness of their desires.

Erfahrung: Considered by Friedrich Nietzsche to be primary knowledge that is learned by doing.

Ethical Relativism: The idea that ethics are a matter of perspective and relative to the norms of a specific culture.

Externality: An economics term that refers to the effect on a third party by a transaction between two other entities. (There can be both positive and negative externalities)

Framing Effects: Decisions influenced by the semantics of

how the options are presented.

Groupthink: A psychological phenomenon that occurs within a group of people in which the desire for harmony or conformity in the group results in an irrational or dysfunctional decision-making outcome (social pressure).

Hawthorne effect: (observer effect) Where individuals modify an aspect of their behavior in response to being observed.

Heterogeneous: Distinctly non-uniform in certain qualities (thought and group members)

Heuristics: Quick problem solving when classic methods are too slow, mental shortcuts

Homogenous: Uniform in composition or character (thought and group members)

Humanist Theory: Rejects the notions of behaviorism that the environment determines the outcome. Favors the notion that human beings can control their own destiny, are inherently good, and desires a better world for themselves and others.

Hygiene Factors: Are job security, salary, fringe benefits, and work conditions. Hygiene factors provide incentives or are a threat to make someone do something and are extrinsic to the job.

Hypothetical Imperatives: Tell us which means best achieve our ends, but they do not tell us which ends we should choose.

<u>Informed Consent</u>: A term used to describe deliberation and free choice.

<u>Injunctive Norms</u>: Behaviors which are perceived as being approved by others (and yourself)

<u>Intelligence quotient (IQ)</u>: Standardized Testing, facts, calculations, logic, formalized reasoning. (see wissen)

<u>Kantian:</u> Goodwill as a universal law for everyone (Immanuel Kant)

<u>Keiretsu</u>: Instead of using bank, a bunch of companies form a group. Then each company in the group borrows money from one another and since they are then interdependent, the companies also consult one another on decisions.

<u>Learning Theory</u>: Cognitive, emotional, and environmental influences, as well as prior experience, all play a part in how understanding, or a world view, is acquired or changed and knowledge and skills retained.

<u>Libertarianism:</u> Personal liberty, and property rights (Robert Nozick)

<u>Longitudinal Survey:</u> A study that involves repeated observations of the same observations over time.

<u>Motivator Factors:</u> Are challenging work, recognition, responsibility, or anything that gives positive satisfaction,

recognition, achievement, or personal growth. Motivators are intrinsic to the job.

Negative Rights: Vital guaranteed rights; like freedom from interference, as well as freedom of speech, religion, and property.

Network Theory: Recognizes communication, formality, proximity, and work flow ties as potential factors in decisions and information flow.

Non-Consequentialist: Prima facie duties based on rational thought (WD Ross)

Personality Theory: The major theories include dispositional (**trait**) perspective, psychodynamic, humanistic, biological, behaviorist, evolutionary and social learning perspective.

Positive Rights: Receiving certain benefits, like education, medical or shelter.

Principal: Is the shareholder and the stakeholders, or whomever the agent is working on behalf of.

Principal-agent Problem: (Agency Theory) Since and agent is able to make decisions on behalf of, and impact another person or entity, there is exists a dilemma when the agent is motivated to act on their own best interests rather than those of the principal.

Psychogenic Needs: A theory based on Maslow's concept of primary and secondary needs, which claims that people are motivated by needs, which will often influence their decisions.

Self-Efficacy Concept: States that all people can identify the things they would like to change.

Shareholder Agency: This agency exults investors over everything else. This ideal believes the sole purpose of a firm is to make money. Anything in conflict with this is doing a disservice to those who provided the money to fund the firm's operations.

Social Contract: Universal equality (John Rawls)

Stakeholders: Primary stakeholders are usually internal, or anyone who might engage in a transaction with the business and secondary stakeholders are considered those affected by the actions of the firm.

Stakeholder Agency: Values both internal and external individuals involved with the company. Internal stakeholders are employees, owners, and managers. External stakeholders are customers, suppliers, government, creditors, society, and also the environment.

Social Theory: Behavior is based on the interactions with others. Social Theory is a combination of Behaviorist and Cognitive theory.

Stoicism: Cerebral in nature, and believed that self-control and mental fortitude could overcome destructive emotions, which was considered to be the root cause for unhappiness. This type of reasoning was disciplined both in action and also in thought.

Teleological Theories: Goals, or ends based ethics, consequentialist motivations.

The Caux Round Table: (CRT) An international organization of senior business executives aiming to promote ethical business practice.

Triple Bottom Line: A catchphrase for accounting for social, environmental, and financial externalities.

Two-Factor/Dual-Factor Theory: (Also known as Herzberg's motivation-hygiene theory) claims there are certain factors in the workplace that are related to job satisfaction (Motivators and Hygiene Factors).

Two-Factor Model of Motivation: This theory suggests that to improve job attitudes and productivity, administrators must recognize and attend to both fundamental needs and psycho-social needs. (See Motivators and Hygiene Factors)

Wissen: Classified by Friedrich Nietzsche as secondary information like books, lectures, and television.

ABOUT THE AUTHOR:

John Endris is a full blown business geek who earned a Bachelor of Science in Business and an MBA from St. Mary's University. He is a business strategy advisor, a serial entrepreneur, active investor, and has an extensive background in the financial services industry.

Made in the USA
Las Vegas, NV
06 September 2021